◆ FriesenPress

One Printers Way
Altona, MB R0G 0B0
Canada

www.friesenpress.com

Police badge vector: Vecteezy.com

ISBN
978-1-03-918855-6 (Hardcover)
978-1-03-918854-9 (Paperback)
978-1-03-918856-3 (eBook)

1. BIOGRAPHY & AUTOBIOGRAPHY, LAW ENFORCEMENT

Distributed to the trade by The Ingram Book Company

I A
reti
be (
Pol
due
at t
alre
mu
at t
ber
also
for

Car
8 p
wo
hos
hat
hor
so l
He
No
As
at t
the

Disclaimer:

This book is based on true events; however, it is not meant to be a memoir. It has been fictionalized to the point that all names of persons appearing in this work are fictitious except for the main character, the writer himself. Names that have any resemblance to real people, living or dead, is entirely coincidental. All incidents are based on true events that have occurred. Some events may not have been placed in the exact chronological order. This has been done to enhance the flow of the works or because the writer believed that it was the actual location and timeframe of the occurrence. The events are told solely from the writer's memory and his point of view. It is the only source for the writing of each incident, the feelings described, and the conversations that took place. There is no intention on behalf of the writer to present any individual in such a way that they may recognize himself or herself with any false or unjust injury. There is no malicious intent to defame, or otherwise slander, the good name of the Force' or its members that I have worked with in the past or present.

I finally got him transferred to Newport Harbour Care Centre, and as soon as I wheeled him into his room, he was all smiles. He finally had a private room, and I was able to hang some of his wonderful paintings to make it more like home. I was living only five minutes away from him. His memory started to improve, and he was smiling a lot and loved his hugs and kisses. In November 2021, I sold the condo that I had moved to as it was much too big for me and bought a smaller condo, still only five minutes away from him. As I am writing this in May 2023, he still remembers me, and he now remembers the kids as well. Even though his speech is mixed up, his eyes and smiles tell a different story.

I must give God all the credit for keeping me strong and giving me such joyous, yet sad, memories. Also, the children and grandchildren have been a blessing and have offered so much help. Thank you so much Julie-Anne and Michael, Ryan and Maria, Kurtis, Colin, and grandchildren Calie-Anne, Alexandra, Luca, Austin, and Elizabeth for keeping me sane throughout the past three years!

I promised him when he went into care, that I would get his book, *Before My Memory Fades: Remembering My Time in the RCMP,* published. I am now keeping my promise to him. I hope you enjoy some of his police stories from 1975 to 1980 when he was transferred to Airdrie Freeway Patrol. It does not include all his stories from his ten years in Airdrie or the last seventeen years of his service when he was transferred to the Forensic Identification Section. Unfortunately, due to his decline in memory, he was unable to complete those stories.

Ivy-Anne Mitchell

Introduction

ONE DECEMBER DAY, I FOUND myself sitting alone in our family room. About six months earlier I had lost a brother to cancer. I realized as I sat there, I was still grieving. Tears filled my eyes as I recalled all the things we did during our younger days as boys in New Brunswick. Steve and I were born a short eleven months apart. This closeness at birth, coupled with the fact that our loving mother had continually dressed us alike, made us feel like twins. Certainly, we were of two very distinct personalities, but from the beginning we remained mysteriously on the same page throughout life. Needless to say, we maintained a great amount of admiration and love for each other.

While sitting there pondering the past, glimpses of our history played vividly in my head. I bounced between tears and laughter, recalling the countless adventures we always seemed to create for ourselves. I knew that I loved him dearly, and that I would miss him the rest of my life.

I mention this because the revival of those bittersweet memories acted as a catalyst to what I am about to tell you. It somehow triggered a review of my *own* life. I began to recall the many incidents that occurred during my career as a peace officer. I immediately set short sentences to paper so I could recount each incident with clarity later. The list first filled one letter-sized sheet, then another, until I had approximately seventy separate stories.

I'm in my senior years now. This book is about my life. During the last two years of my career, I was diagnosed with Parkinson's disease. Despite the newest medications, the disease still forced me to retire during the early months of 2007. I have since learned to accept and cope with it, as I had no other choice.

In most ways, I'm like any other average Canadian grandfather, filled with unconditional love for his wife and grandchildren. I certainly love spending time with all of them. The following collection of stories and events are about my life as a thirty-two-year veteran of the Royal Canadian Mounted Police. It's about the types of events that shaped my character into what I've become today. They are simple experiences and nothing more. Regardless of that fact, they have left an indelible mark on my psyche.

I've had both good and bad experiences while working with the "Force." For the most part, I've enjoyed life as a Mountie. It was a life that sent me to nine different detachments in five different provinces while performing eight specific duties. It was an experience filled with excitement and danger, but most of all, with personal satisfaction. Whether my life experiences had been created by design or by chance, I can only conjecture. I will probably never know. One thing is certain; it was a wonderful, interesting life.

Although I hadn't obtained great rank nor received many awards and accolades during my career, I do remember many proud moments. Those were the moments that change my life and the lives of others in a positive way.

The stories I've compiled are based on true events. They were written solely from my point of view. To my friends and colleagues that read this book, I make no excuses for how I have described events or individual characters in any of its contents. The stories have been written from my memory without the use of notes or a diary. I have relentlessly endeavoured to ensure nothing else has been added to purposely enhance or embellish. Therefore, I present the events of my career as a proud retired member of the Royal Canadian Mounted Police.

I began my career as a twenty-three-year-old idealistic individual. I joined the Royal Canadian Mounted Police on the second of June 1975. Just prior to my police career, I had been working as a machinist with the Canadian National Railway. Up to that time, I had been exposed to a moderate array of life experiences. I regarded myself as neither naïve nor gullible. I had experienced some special events in my late teens that had a positive effect on my confidence level. By twenty-three, I felt I could carry out most tasks with minimal initial guidance before completing the task successfully.

When looking back to 1967, at the age of sixteen I was proud of my accomplishments. I had earned a private pilot licence flying 1964 vintage Piper Cherokees at the Moncton Flying Club. The next year, I received another scholarship from the Canadian Air Force Reserve Program to obtain a glider pilot licence at the air force base in Greenwood, Nova Scotia. In those two years, I learned the value of courage, camaraderie, teamwork, a reliance on personal judgement, responsibility for other's equipment, and the dangers of making the one simple mistake of inattentiveness.

In addition, I had received some military training as a private, then as a reserve second lieutenant in the Armoured Corp, specifically the Eighth Canadian Hussars, a New Brunswick regiment. I found I enjoyed the military training and experiences very much. I was taught to march and drive all types of military vehicles, from jeeps to tanks and everything in between. Some of the subjects I valued the most included courses on survival; the use of camouflage, escape and evade; map-reading; and stealthy methods to move vehicles and troops across country while avoiding detection, to name a few. By far, the most invaluable segment of my military training I received related to the handling of handguns, rifles, and machine guns. "Safety First" and safe handling of a loaded or unloaded weapon had been ingrained in me. Later, as a policeman, that factor was always an issue when attempting to control a violent scene whether it was about to occur, was occurring, or had already occurred.

The military experience also indoctrinated me with a valuable concept. In a nutshell, it thrust the full responsibility on me when I received a mission or task to complete. It reinforced confidence and duty, as regardless of the barriers that stood in my path, the mission had to be completed successfully. Of course, as a soldier I thought of it in the extreme since I believed it meant it was my duty to complete a mission at any cost.

Although I somewhat embraced it as a peace officer, the common-sense part of me never believed that all missions or tasks should be completed at any cost. That type of thinking was too extreme. It seemed ludicrous to me. It may have been fine for a soldier, but as a policeman, I gravitated towards a modified version. I would use the personal strength generated by the concept only in a situation of life or death for a victim or myself.

I was not always successful in all my endeavours at work, but using that concept, even in its mildest form, did make most incidents turn out without failure. I practiced "thinking outside the box," to use all the ingenuity I could muster to solve the crime or complete a file success-fully. I taught myself to always be on guard for the unexpected. It had the positive effect of making me more prepared for what police work was all about—people and how they reacted to one another.

I had been taught while growing up that it was right to defend the kids that I saw being picked on and to never be afraid of being different. Different in colour, or custom, or nationality, as all of us were human and all our lives had value. I learned to accept persons that had disabilities, both physical and mental, for they had value as human beings too. These beliefs were reinforced time after time throughout my life and police career. In fact, one of my best witnesses in a hit and run case had been a man who suffered brain damage during an earlier shooting. Without his poignant testimony, we wouldn't have convicted the culprit. Most of all, I had been taught to be proud of knowing people of different cultures, languages, and customs. My family always believed there were good and bad persons in all cultures. Their philosophy in life was about learning how to cope with the good and evil in man. Each encounter should be used to learn to recognize the good ones from the bad ones. The events of my childhood and early adulthood had shaped me into a person with definite beliefs of what was good and what was evil. In that sense, I naturally gravitated towards a career in police work, but specially to the RCMP.

I had always taken my job as a peace officer very seriously. I was proud to serve the Canadian people as a Mountie. I did my best to always remain fair and honest. I continually endeavoured to stay within the accepted legal boundaries of the law throughout my career. I strove to never use violence as the first resort to subdue or diffuse an incident. Although, as many members can tell you, violence is always present, and it happens frequently when the police meet complainants and bad guys alike.

I've known those members who loved the fight and the confrontations, but they are in the minority. Most members believe as I believe, the use of violence should be our last resort. There are extreme circumstances when violence must be used. At events when a peace officer's duty dictates, he must preserve his own life, the victim's life, those of innocent bystanders, and even the bad guy's life.

By joining the Force, I understood those concepts and once I became a member, I tried to maintain a consistent approach to people in general.

I've gone through those earlier experiences only to help you understand my character and the impetus that made me become a member of the Force.

Like most young boys of the fifties, I grew up with heroes like the Lone Ranger, Superman, Red Rider, and The Mounties of the Royal Canadian Mounted Police. To become one of those heroes was all my friends and I would think about as we played together.

Like all great imaginary things, eventually those childish dreams faded into reality. It turned out I became a machinist with the railroad. A job I had foolishly taken to please my father.

I was always keenly aware early in life that dreams could sometimes come true, but as time passed working as a machinist, I became more of a skeptic than a believer of such fairy tales. I discovered that "wanting something" and "getting it" were two separate things that very rarely met. The dreams finally disappeared and a railroad machinist I became.

After working in that field for two years something seemed to be missing for me. Although I could do the job without much difficulty, I realized it wasn't for me. It became a routine rut that trapped me with no way out of it.

Approximately three long years had passed when a chance circumstance caused a re-awakening of my childhood dream. It presented itself from a most unlikely source. The timing seemed right. I was a few years older and ready to take action to obtain my goal. It happened to be one of my father's habits that sparked the opportunity. The story is a bit strange, so I'd like to dwell on it for a few minutes.

CHAPTER 1

First Contact

IT WAS A SUMMER DAY in 1974. My father had just arrived home from work. As was his custom, before anything else, he always washed up first. We waited for him to walk directly into our small living room where he began settling down in his personal rocking chair. He was trying to read the newspaper. Without even looking at him, I could hear that familiar rustling sound the pages made as he struggled continuously to adjust it to his own comfort level.

He suddenly began to read aloud to us all. He pointed out an article that indicated the Royal Canadian Mounted Police was looking for auxiliary constables. For those who don't know—an auxiliary constable is a civilian who has limited training, wore the police uniform, and worked on a volunteer basis to assist regular members with police duties.

I was secretly interested, but my father and I weren't quite getting along that day due to an argument about some silly thing the night before. I remained silent and coy. My father looked directly at me as he read aloud. I knew he was trying to ascertain if I was interested. I didn't react, or at least I don't think he could tell I was really very interested.

That night, after the paper had been discarded, I read the entire article in the confines of my bedroom to gather as much information as possible. The more I read the more I liked the idea of becoming a part-time policeman. The article specifically stated that the RCMP was looking for interested members of the public to volunteer once or twice a month as auxiliary constables.

Instructions were given to attend the office so the names of any potential candidates could be placed on a waiting list. I viewed it as an opportunity to get some police experience and to really find out if the career was what I believed it to be.

I told no one of my plans. A day later I drove to the RCMP subdivision building in Moncton to apply as an auxiliary constable. At the very least, I just wanted my name on the list.

As soon as I entered the building I was amazed at the brightness of the shiny floors and the sense of order that permeated the air. But I was especially impressed with the constable that politely greeted me as we passed in the hallway. He was wearing his red serge, high brown boots, riding breaches, and a Stetson. The jingling sound of his silver spurs as he walked past me confirmed that I was in the right place.

I stood in awe of my surroundings as I walked up to an open counter area. A well-dressed female clerk appeared. She took my request for assistance. I readily waited patiently, soaking up the surroundings like a drug addict enjoying every second of a trip. Little did I know, a few short minutes later that state of euphoria would end abruptly.

I listened eagerly to the woman's response as she returned. I could tell she was a professional and a kind-hearted employee by the way she delivered her response to my request.

"Corporal Todd oversees the Auxiliary Constable Program. He is available now. If you step inside, I'll take you to his office." She opened the inner office door and I eagerly stepped through the threshold.

I followed her—like every young man, I admired the view. As I entered the corporal's office, I was motioned to sit down on a hard maple wooden armchair. It seemed to be positioned to ensure that any visitors had to face the corporal from directly across his desk.

I whispered, "Thank-you," as the woman left me sitting there.

I looked at the middle-aged corporal. He was wearing his regular RCMP street uniform with his head turned away. He was speaking on the phone while reaching into a lower desk drawer. I watched as he turned towards me with a file folder in his right hand. As our eyes met his conversation sort of halted. He said something then hung up the phone. He stared directly at me for a moment from the other side of his desk, a mere four feet away. His expression was surprisingly serious. The sudden silence made me feel uncomfortable, so I spoke first.

"Corporal Todd? I'm Tim Mitchell. I've come in to see you about the Auxiliary Constable Program. I'd like to put my name on the list—if I could?"

He remained silent for a few more seconds then leaned back into his chair.

Stubborn to the Bone

THE SHORT WAIT WAS ENDED when he fired out his first question to me. "Do you have a motorcycle?"

"No, Sir."

I had been caught completely off guard. In a split-second many thoughts went through my head. At first, I struggled to comprehend the unexpected question. I couldn't figure out why it was asked. I thought, *What was wrong with asking my name, where I lived, or what I did for a living? Or even why was I interested? Like some of the normal questions I had expected.*

Within the few seconds of silence, I managed to look down at my jacket. It was styled like a motorcycle jacket, and it was black.

I suddenly started to get it, so I answered, "No, I don't. I have a car. Its outside—it's a Mercury Montclair."

He shot out another question as quickly as I answered, "Have you ever been a member of a motorcycle gang?"

I was taken back once again by this second question. My mind raced *Does he really think that because I have a leather jacket on that I'm a gang member?*

In retrospect, I guess it wasn't easy for me to believe that he just couldn't plainly see that I was a good guy who honestly admired the police and just wanted to volunteer to help. It almost made my blood boil, but I knew it was important not to get angry or to react in any inappropriate way when answering his questions.

During the few more seconds that followed, thoughts went through my head to reassure myself, I've never even been stopped by the police nor had I any problems with the law during my entire lifetime!

I took a breath and answered in my politest tone, "No, I've never had anything to do with motorcycle gangs—I don't even own a motorcycle. I just liked this leather jacket, so I bought it some time ago."

He kept looking directly at me. I sensed that for some reason, he didn't believe me. The corporal's stance left me in shock. I desperately wanted him to believe me when I said I wasn't some sort of biker.

I automatically responded in a more defensive tone. "I work as a machinist with the railway, I've never been in trouble—all I want to do is help the police by volunteering as an auxiliary constable. Is it possible for you to put my name on your list?"

"I have no more room on the list! I can't take your name! Our list if full for the next two years! Thanks for coming in. Have a good day!

He stood up and reached out his hand as if bidding me to leave. I instinctively stood up and shook his hand in response. I somehow angered him, and I didn't know why!

I stopped abruptly just outside his office door. Before I could take another step, I had to ask him once more. So, I turned to him and opened my mouth, "You just can't put my name on your waiting list? If it takes two years, that's all right. I'm not going anywhere, and I would like to help!"

He barked back a response, "No! I can't put you on the list! That's all I have to say on the matter. GOOD DAY!"

With that curt response I had no choice but to follow him to the exit door. From my first step outside, the shock and disappointment got progressively more intense. The further I walked away the more my disappointment turned into anger. I couldn't believe how I had been treated. I began to reason with myself, *I don't think he even listened to my name—so how could he be able to judge whether I was a candidate or not? He didn't even open his file folder to check just how many persons were on the list.* I spent the rest of the trip home in a quandary as to how to handle his outright rejection.

It was the only the second time any RCMP member had ever spoken to me. It left a bad taste in my mouth. In those long moments, the idea of volunteering for them was wiped cleanly from my mind.

It wasn't until several days had passed before I dealt with the matter again. I began thinking about the corporal's attitude and how it made me feel. I've never been one to give up easily. I was taught that perseverance was the key to success so I decided I would have to pursue it further. I was determined not to let one bad individual's attitude spoil my belief in the members of the Royal Canadian Mounted Police. Maybe it was my pride or just my anger that compelled me to act. To this day, I still really don't know.

Part of me began to reconcile his actions by telling myself, *Maybe he just had a bad day? Better yet, maybe there was someone else other than Corporal Todd to deal with the matter?*

With that small ray of hope my spirits were lifted. I decided too again. I've always had a problem accepting the answer "No!" When someone says, "You can't do it!" I say, "Let's try!" It was something our father had instilled in me.

The act of becoming an auxiliary constable suddenly went to the forefront of my plans. I was determined to overcome the corporal's prejudices one way or the other. I patiently waited two more weeks before returning to the subdivision building. I walked up to the main counter and asked for Corporal Todd once more. This time I was wearing my best casual clothes and the appropriate jacket along with a fresh haircut and my shiniest shoes. The same woman looked at me as if we hadn't met before. At the same time, she seemed to recognize that there was something familiar about me.

She asked my name then asked if I'd been there before. I confirmed that it was my second time. That response seemed to leave her even more puzzled. After a few moments, Corporal Todd appeared at the front counter. He seemed to be more congenial at first. He wasn't frowning or so serious when he spoke, "What can I do for you today?" I was sure then that he hadn't remembered my name or at least hadn't recognized me.

I naively answered, "I'm wondering if anything has changed on your list of auxiliary constables? I'm still interested in having my name placed on the list, Sir!"

His face changed as he realized who it was standing before him. He even remembered my name.

"Look, Mitchell, I told you some time ago that I'm not putting you on the list! Stop wasting my time! Good day!" He turned and quickly walked away into his office then slammed the door.

I looked at the female clerk after Corporal Todd's outburst, and she looked at me. I instinctively spoke to her, "I wonder what his problem is? All I want to do is to volunteer by helping the police."

She looked at me sympathetically but said nothing. I tried to pretend that everything was fine. I cheerfully gave her an additional response.

"I hope you have a good day anyway!" I walked out of the building thinking to myself, I *guess that's strike two! What a jerk he is!*

I know it sounded like his second rejection should have really affected me. Well, it did, it hurt me even more than the first encounter. The more I thought about it the more it made me angry inside. I kept thinking, *What a stubborn man! Letting his hidden prejudices prevent me from volunteering to help. I knew I was honest and a hard worker. I've never been in trouble with the law. I hadn't even had a speeding ticket! Why couldn't he see that?*

I refused to believe a problem like that could even exist and I decided I had to share my dilemma with someone.

Once at home again, I told my younger brother, Steve about it. After getting his advice, I swore him to silence. I didn't want anyone else in the family to know until I succeeded.

CHAPTER 3

A New Direction

MY CONVERSATION WITH STEVE HAD stimulated a plan to circumvent the corporal completely. I made a call to the RCMP office. I recognized the voice on the phone to be the same female employee that met me on the two previous occasions. I engaged her help to arrange a meeting with the Force's full-time recruiter. I crossed my fingers hoping it wouldn't be Corporal Todd.

I was in luck. It turned out to be a Constable Grier. He was a younger member with about five years of service. I asked the clerk on the phone if it was possible to schedule a meeting with Constable Grier when Corporal Todd wasn't there, considering his attitude towards me. To my surprise, she readily cooperated. She didn't seem to like Corporal Todd very much either. With her assistance, the meeting was scheduled to occur in eight days.

When the anxious day finally came, I got dressed as before. This time I really wanted to impress the recruiter. I double-checked that I had all my personal information. Records of my past experiences and qualifications were with me and available for disclosure. I wanted to look prepared, confident, and certain for the recruiter to assure him of my decision to join the Force.

I re-entered the main entrance of the RCMP building for the third time with some trepidation. I didn't want to run into Corporal Todd again. The woman smiled when she saw me standing at the counter. Without saying a word, she stood up. I watched her walk into another office a short distance to the right of where I was standing.

Within a very short time, Constable Grier appeared at the counter. He was a tall, blonde man in his late twenties. I noticed he was out of uniform, wearing casual civilian clothes. He shook my hand immediately. I noticed a difference from my contact with the corporal. I could tell his handshake was genuinely friendly. He seemed very upbeat and happy to be there. His demeanour immediately made me feel welcome.

As we walked the short distance to his office, he had already found out my name, where I lived, where I worked, and some additional family and sibling information. The conversation flowed freely between us. I remember thinking, *This guy is great! I could really see him as a friend. I want to treat everyone like he does! He's great!*

Then it was down to business. I told him everything about my attempts to get Corporal Todd to put me on that auxiliary constable list and his reactions to it. I said, "I've had about a month to think it all over. I've concluded that I'd rather be a full-time peace officer instead of a part-time volunteer. I am seriously interested in joining the Force as a regular member."

Constable Grier was a nice guy and a professional. He assured me that Corporal Todd would have nothing to do with my application being accepted or denied. He was my recruiter and no one else. He further explained if I passed the standard entrance tests, had a clean record, and otherwise passed the background investigation, I would most likely be a viable candidate to join the Force.

I was relieved and very happy at the outcome of the first interview. I received all the application forms before heading on my way. He also warned me there were many obstacles to overcome when applying as a regular member. He reiterated that even for outstanding candidates, problems getting in could sometimes surface. Constable Grier said,

"Remember, Tim, this is only the beginning of a long process. Keep your chin up. If everything is as you say it is, everything will work out fine."

I was extremely excited. I remember bouncing out of there with a smile from ear to ear. During my drive home, I reminded myself that this would remain a secret until I got accepted.

The next few months became a hectic blur of activity. The list of required and suggested activities seemed enormous at times. I surreptitiously arranged the required medical tests and gathered my relatives' background information to complete the basic application forms. Once compiled, the information was promptly returned to Constable Grier for processing. The next step would be the exams that already had been scheduled for the following week.

I successfully completed the required written entrance tests. I began the continuous physical regimen my recruiter had suggested. I familiarized myself with all the recommended materials and books. I read and trained secretly while still maintaining my full-time job as a machinist. I was tired but deep down very excited. A positive feeling that I may have a real chance to attain the dream filled my heart.

Suddenly the childhood dream of becoming a Mountie was a tangible possibility. By the end of the second month everything had been completed. A phone call from Constable Grier revealed, "The waiting game is now on. Your background investigation hasn't been completed yet. It's been given to the plainclothes unit, and I have no control over how fast they can get it done."

He assured me, "If you've been honest about everything in your previous interviews you should be fine! All you can do is to wait for a phone call from the division recruitment representative. He'll give you the final answer."

I hung up the phone with a feeling of uncertainty. *Had I told them everything*? I racked my brain over and over, but I couldn't think of anything else.

I've been honest with everything! I'm sure I have. The days passed and the self-imposed physical training continued. The daily routine of exercising, eating, sleeping, and attending to my job became a ritual. I still hadn't told anyone about my application, except my brother.

This brought on thoughts of my mother's feelings. To say her first-born child was special to her was an understatement. At times, I could do no wrong in her eyes. I think she always knew that I was grateful to her for that "prized position." Her support for me remained unwavering throughout my life. In the days to follow, I found myself thinking about how she might be affected by the news of me becoming a member. I knew she'd be proud of me and afraid for my safety at the same time. I visualized the torment of her worrying continuously about me being shot or injured. I didn't want to hurt her in any way, but the dream of joining was so strong it seemed to unevenly balance those concerns towards joining the Force. Nevertheless, I avoided thinking about it as much as possible.

Of course, being young, I thought, *nothing could happen*. I persisted in thinking, *it was all just an adventure. I'd be fine whatever happened.*

The days that followed soon grew into two months. I waited patiently without any word from Constable Grier.

I had just been placed on a new shift at work. I began working the midnight to 8:00 a.m. shift. It was a hard shift to get used to at first. I found myself sleeping until 2:00 p.m. each day. This put a large cramp into my exercise regimen. I found I was tired all the time. I became kind of lethargic. The situation went on for several more months until the dream of becoming a Mountie turned into a distant vision increasingly blurred by the lack of response from the Force. Still, I was able to keep the secret.

The plan I had to surprise Corporal Todd had long faded into memory. I began to settle for the conclusion that none of it mattered at all. I was almost resigned to the fact I would be a machinist the rest of my life. I convinced myself it wasn't that bad after all.

So, there I was living at home with no steady girlfriend, in a boring job, without the gumption to change a thing. *Could it get any worse*?

It was a new state of mind for me. I had never been depressed in my whole life. I should have instinctively kicked myself back into positive action. Complacency was not in my nature. I struggled without success to pull out of the comfortable routine of eat, sleep, and work. It was like a thick cocoon that began to smother any chance of change. It all seemed hopeless.

One morning about four months later, I was awakened abruptly from a deep sleep by my mother. I had just finished falling asleep after another hard midnight shift. I looked at my clock as I groaned and rolled over. It was 9:15 a.m. I struggled with great effort to wake up, so I could comprehend what she was saying to me. I finally heard her say "Someone is on the phone for you—it's the RCMP!"

My internal lights went on, bells and whistles sounded in my head. Suddenly being tired was not an issue. I was up and walking very fast to the phone. I didn't realize it until later, but my mother thought I was in trouble with the police for some reason.

I picked up the phone and in a raspy voice I said, "Hello, this is Tim Mitchell—can I help you?"

I have never forgotten the words spoken by the unknown voice "Are you ready to attend Fredericton Division Headquarters on June 2nd, 1975, at 10:00 a.m. for the purpose of engagement into the Force?"

I went silent, and then answered with disbelief, "Yes! Yes, I am!" Then I paused and quickly asked the voice a question. "Can you tell me what you said again please?" The voice repeated the question exactly.

I answered, "Yes, I am! Thank you! Thank you very much! Good-bye!" I hung up the phone. I was definitely wide awake by then. I looked at my mother as she looked at me. I saw questions and concerns in her face. I knew she wanted to hear why the police had called me.

I hugged her and said, "I'm going into the RCMP! They want me to get engaged in the Force on June 2nd in Fredericton!" Simultaneously we were both elated. I was determined not to go back to sleep. My mind was churning with all the things I had to do before June 2nd. It was the first day of May. I had less than a month to quit my job, to get my financial affairs in order, and have someone take care of my car. Then there was the problem of getting back into shape to prepare for training.

I wanted to tell everyone my long-kept secret. I was so happy that I called into work that day to notify them I was taking the next shift off. Then my mother took over the phone. Within a few minutes my mother notified every possible person in the family, her friends, and all of our neighbours with the news. She even notified people that hadn't known me at all.

It was a proud time for me. The month of May was one of the quickest months of my life. By the time June came along, I had miraculously gotten everything in order. I was packed and ready to go. Constable Grier contacted me with further instructions shortly after the unknown voice called. He stated that at my earliest convenience, I would have to attend the Moncton office to have my photograph and another set of fingerprints taken as part of joining the Force. He said he'd be away for the next week. To facilitate matters he would leave my file with the front counter clerk so anyone working could help me.

I wanted to stay on top of everything, so I headed down to the office the very next morning. I wore my leather jacket this time. I walked into the now familiar front entrance, directly up to the counter. The same woman was working at her desk. She knew my name by that time. She raised her head and smiled. She approached the front counter with my file in her hands She said, "Tim, is it alright if Corporal Todd takes your fingerprints and photograph? There's no one else here right now or would you prefer to come back tomorrow?"

I thought for a second then replied, "No, it should be fine."

She went on to explain almost whispering, "He doesn't really like you as you know? And he doesn't know you're joining. Constable Grier hasn't told him anything about it."

The more I thought about it the more I was agreeable to having him do it. "This should be good!" I thought. So, it was agreed, she would take me to the dreaded Corporal Todd's office allowing me to carry my own file to present to him. I could tell by the way she looked at me that she was going to enjoy it—maybe just as much as I would?

I must admit I was a bit nervous, not knowing what type of reaction I would receive from Todd. The bitter taste left in my memory by his prejudiced treatment towards me was still very strong. After all, he did nothing less than throw me out of his office more than once.

Halfway across the inner office floor I could see the frown on Corporal Todd's face as he saw the clerk escorting me to his location. A few steps further, I'm sure I could hear him say to himself, "What do you want now?"

It was too late. We were in his office. I stood precariously, silently awaiting any type of reaction from my presence. The clerk announced me, indicating that Constable Grier requested that he assist me by taking my photograph and a set of fingerprints to complete my engagement requirements.

"The instructions are in the file," she stated. I blinked, then she was gone, leaving an open-mouthed corporal almost falling off his wooden swivel chair. He seemed to turn a little pale and for several moments said nothing. I purposely laid the file in front of him on the desk.

He knew very well that Constable Grier processed candidates to become regular members of the Force. I'm sure he realized that I was not there to bother him about volunteering. He began to react. He stood up, picked up the file and said politely, "Can you give me a minute? I'll be right back!"

"Sure!" I replied as I felt my insides wanting to burst out into laughter. I kept covering my mouth in an effort to prevent it from happening for about the next five minutes.

To take my mind off the laughter, I looked around Corporal Todd's office during his absence. I noticed his desk was clean, his books and manuals were neatly stored in an exact order in the bookcases. His garbage can was empty, and even his coat seemed to be hung precisely on the coat rack behind his desk. Nothing at all was out of place. I'm no clean freak but I had to admire him for that at least. I thought for a second then puzzled, *Maybe that's why he was so angry—having to keep everything in order all of the time—it must take its toll on one's psyche?*

Before I could think anymore, he returned, saying, "Tim! Come with me, we're going to take your fingerprints and take a photograph or two." I got up and followed him to the guardroom where I removed my jacket and rolled up my sleeves preparing to get inked for fingerprinting. The process was performed without incident. The corporal said nothing.

After I had washed my hands and signed three copies of my fingerprints, he suggested where I should stand so he could take a photograph. A couple of snaps later it was completed.

He looked at me and then spoke in a controlled, almost monotone voice, "You can go. I'll give the completed file to Constable Grier. Everything will be fine. Good luck with your career choice."

I thanked him and stuck out my hand. He shook it then motioned for me to follow him out to the front of the office. When I stepped on the other side of the counter, I turned back to say something, but he had disappeared. The clerk was sitting at her desk. We both found ourselves smiling. She winked at me and said, "Good luck Tim." I thanked her and left the building. The only thing I still regret was never asking the lovely lady's name.

Her kindness, her smile, and especially the unexpected help she had so freely given me to get into the Force was clearly burned into my memory from that time on.

CHAPTER

4

Leaving Home

THAT FINAL MONTH, I SAID all my good-byes to friends and co-workers. I was very excited, and everyone could tell. Each of them wished me luck in their own special way. I felt as if I were on top of the world. I received my unexpected accolades. It had all felt a little strange. I hadn't even been sworn in nor had I received any training. Yet there I was being treated as a Mountie.

It all felt good, but I was never really fooled into believing that I was a real Mountie. I knew it was just the beginning. There would be many trials and challenges that would test my very mettle before I could really call myself a Mountie. I could only imagine the experience-filled journey that lay ahead. It would be a journey where I would have to use all my capabilities and training to prove my personal worth.

It was the beginning of a new life, away from home, on my own in a career that had already filled me with position and pride.

I was determined to search out the attributes and strengths I required to be the type of peace officer others would look up to as one of the best.

The day came to leave for Fredericton, New Brunswick. My father drove my mother, one sister, and me to the Division Headquarters to be sworn in as a peace officer by the Commanding Officer of "J" Division. My six other siblings were disappointed that they couldn't attend. They were either out of the country or had other commitments.

After an hour on the road, I soon realized my family seemed more affected by my new career choice than I had been. The chatter and questions were non-stop the whole trip. My mother must have told me at least a thousand times how much she loved me. Like typical Easterners, they really didn't want to their eldest son to leave home. I guessed their real fear was I would never come back.

After the swearing-in ceremony, we all shook hands then posed for the usual photograph or two. Once the rituals were over, I was given a hotel reservation and airline tickets. My plane would leave for Regina early the next morning. I thanked the assistant commissioner before leaving the building with my sister and parents. Outside I said my good-byes to my family amid a flurry of smiles and tears. Each sentiment taking its turn subduing the other, until I watched my father's car drive away.

It wasn't until the next morning, while standing in the waiting area at the tiny Fredericton Airport, that I realized that I was not alone. I was dressed in the recommended clothing, a pair of dress slacks, shirt, and tie with a sports jacket. Something we all call casual business attire.

I looked around at the almost twenty perspective passengers. Five other males of my age were dressed very closely to what I was wearing. All of them with short hair and a familiar look—the look of anticipation and excitement. I thought to myself, *we must all be heading to the same location.* I was eager to find out.

I walked to the closest potential candidate and asked, "Hi! Where are you heading?"

He proudly and very quickly answered, "Regina, Depot Division, for training. What about you?

Of course, you know what I replied. Within minutes all of us had met each other. It was not surprising that my new friends were all fellow New Brunswickers. Two of us were from Moncton, two from Saint John, and two from around the Fredericton area. We were all around the same age, early twenties, and we were all proud and excited. An easy bond was created with each of them in the days and months that would follow.

When beginning this project, I told myself that I wouldn't go into detail about Depot Division and the six months of training. I believe those first six months in training would fill another book entirely. It would be adequate to say it was a place where boys became men. A place where an individual's mettle was tested, where lifelong comrades were developed, but most of all where we each received the permanent invisible brand marking us as being members of the Royal Canadian Mounted Police.

I had successfully overcome the many hurdles that were presented during training at Depot Division in Regina. Following the graduation celebrations, the real challenges were about to begin. After six months of training in an enclosed system where mistakes in procedures and misinterpretations of knowledge were forgiven, the day came to meet the real world while embracing life as a Mountie in its entirety. From that safe place, I began the role of a peace officer by accepting my first posting, Vermilion, Alberta. It was time to bite the bullet and test what I had learned.

Before leaving Depot, I had a clear understanding that the public trusted our every word in 1975. I took this very seriously. I knew it was not to be abused. This concept may be seen as naïve by today's standards. I think it's because no one trusts anything or anyone anymore. Back then, it was a pleasure to be trusted and believed, both in court and on the street. Armed with that idealistic view and a .38 calibre revolver, I prepared to leave Depot Division the next morning.

CHAPTER 5

My First Posting in Alberta

EARLY ON THE SECOND OF December 1975, in Regina, I hopped on a Greyhound bus heading for the town of Vermilion. The trip would take seven and a half hours. I had been sitting beside the same passenger the whole time. She was an older woman named Peggy Wilkinson. To pass the time we had both talked up a storm.

I never had any problems talking to women, so the time elapsed rather quickly. We seemed to trust each other from our first few words. We found ourselves relating stories about our lives that we wouldn't have normally told strangers. The conversation shortened the boring drive immensely. When we approached the end of the trip and when we were close to the Alberta border, the driver announced the next stop would Lloydminster.

When the bus pulled into the depot, our conversation came to an end. That was where Peggy got off the bus. She got up and leaned over to give me a hug. She then said, "Thanks for the conversation and good luck in Vermilion!"

I replied with a simple, "Thanks!"

I sat in my seat and continued to watch her walking away through the window. Before entering the bus depot, she abruptly stopped and turned back once. She noticed that I was still watching her. In response she smiled, waved, and then disappeared into the building.

I found out so many things about her on that bus trip. She had spoken about her children. Facts like out of her six children, two had died in the Korean War, one had become a dentist, and three were farming in the Lloydminster area. Her husband had been killed in a motor vehicle accident while driving over a blind hill four miles from their farm ten years ago. And most important, she had an Australian Shepherd called Misty that she loved almost more than life itself.

I remember having an odd feeling as the bus drove away. It was like I had just waved to an old friend who was leaving for good. I paused to think, *I sure hope I get to see and talk to her again? I like her; she's a nice lady. She reminds me of my own mom.*

During that final leg of the trip my mind finally returned to the task at hand. I went over everything I knew about Vermilion. When the posting assignment list first came out in the middle of training, both my instructors and troop-mates alike laughed at the choice. They all thought I was posted to *Fort Vermilion* in northern Alberta. Some members regarded it as a less than desirable first posting. That fact may have been true in those days, but experience has since taught me that all postings are good if you have the right frame of mind. Remember home is where you hang your hat—a Stetson in my case.

So, to quell my concern, I rushed to the closest map to see where it was located. When I found both Vermilion and Fort Vermilion on the map, I was relieved.

Vermilion was really located on the Trans-Canada Highway approximately 120 miles east of Edmonton, Alberta, and thirteen miles southwest of Lloydminster, Saskatchewan. It was a municipality of about 3,300 people. Its main industry base was mixed farming and oil exploration. The real laugh was on them.

It was a sergeant's detachment with twelve to thirteen members working on municipal, rural, and highway patrol duties. There was one female office clerk and one permanent guard. When thinking back now, it was the very best place to begin my career. Both the town site and the rural areas were fairly quiet, filled with an abundance of good people. Best of all I was afforded the necessary time to learn the craft of policing.

During those final three months of training, I had also found out my accommodations would be in the barracks of the detachment office building. It was very common for new single members to be billeted that way in the 1970s and 80s.

For those who are unaware of just how barrack living was set up, I'll explain. The RCMP detachment buildings of the time were all built using the same basic floor plans with subtle difference depending upon specific needs. The police office and guardroom-cell area took up about half of the building.

Attached within the same structure were two living accommodation areas. One was an area designated for the member in charge of the detachment and his family. That portion had the same style of rooms as a small house with a living room, kitchen, and so on.

Located between the office portion and the Commander's portion was a separate room or two set aside as accommodation for single members. At any given time, several members could be billeted together while sharing those same spartan facilities. Most barracks contained only one main bedroom, one bathroom, and one other common room that was used as a relaxation area. It acted as a gathering point for the barrack occupants to socialize, play games, eat, and generally interact with each other while off-duty. Most often, each barracks had its own entrance to allow some sense of privacy.

It wasn't until the last few kilometres on the bus that I suddenly came to a surprising realization. I had been mentally preparing to live in Vermilion during the past three months of training. I had already accepted it as my new home and new posting—without ever being in Vermilion before. I found that a strange anxiousness suddenly came over me. I was entering my first posting.

I thought, *I wasn't just driving in as a soldier or even a machinist, but as a peace officer. I was a representative of the National Police Force of Canada whose sole duty was to "Maintain the Right," to be fair and just, to be honest, and most of all to be the protector of all who abided there.* I smiled as I secretly enjoyed that proud moment.

I looked up and saw that my trip was ending. The bus had just driven passed the Town of Vermilion sign. The commercial buildings and the grain elevators loomed into view. I eagerly looked back and forth through all the windows trying to locate the bus depot.

As we crossed the railroad tracks and began entering the main downtown area, I suddenly located it with the aid of the conspicuously parked Mounted Police car. It was parked at an angle that straddled two reserved lanes designated for busses only.

A dark-haired male member in uniform began to get out just as we pulled up. I watched him as he stared purposefully at the bus in his dark sunglasses.

When I heard the sound of the air brakes I stood up, grabbed my jacket, and prepared to disembark. It was a bright sunny day—a nice day to arrive at a new post. The instant I stepped down from the bus, Constable Tig Mason walked directly up to me. I was picked out of all the other passengers right away. He greeted me and we mutually introduced ourselves. I was astonished at first.

How did he know who I was?

I had momentarily forgotten about the way I identified the other candidates at the Fredericton Airport a mere six months earlier.

Constable Mason used the same thought process, I'm sure it had been easy to recognize me. I was the only shorthaired male wearing a suit coat with a tie. In the mid-seventies, most people travelling on a bus wore clothes that were slightly reminiscent of the hippy era in the sixties. Young men had longer hair on their heads and on their faces. Bell-bottom trousers and shirts with bolder and more colourful patterns were in. Even my issued black oxford shoes were a give-away. I would have to say I easily stood out from the rest.

I looked around while joining in the line-up of passengers awaiting their luggage to be removed from the base of the bus. We all juggled for position as the driver began to pull pieces of our luggage out, then carelessly tossed them to the ground helter-skelter.

Tig and I couldn't say much beyond the introduction in the crowd. He grabbed one of my suitcases and I grabbed the other one. He placed it in the back seat on the driver's side of the car. I followed suit with the other one.

Once he started to drive off, we began to talk. He was direct and friendly. My first impression was that I liked him.

He quickly explained the barracks set up. He went on to say, "There will be three of us in barracks with you here now. Bryce Calder is the other member with us. You'll like him. He's a good guy—I imagine the trip from Regina was long and boring considering it's mostly prairie?"

"No, surprisingly it didn't seem too long. I sat beside an older lady who kept me entertained with her life story for most of the trip. Unfortunately, she got off in Lloydminster."

"A lady's man eh! Better be careful out here. They marry mighty easy—no matter what age they are!" Tig laughed when he saw my silent reaction.

The conversation came to a halt. Tig had stopped our police car very close to the detachment's main front door. Before I could move, the main door opened. A very large round sergeant came over to my side of the car. He pulled my door opened and stuck out his hand.

I climbed out, shaking his hand while he spoke. "I'm Sergeant Tibber. I see Constable Mason has picked you up all right. Welcome to Vermilion! Come right into my office and bring your papers so we can get down to business."

He didn't give me time to say anything. So, I followed him, remembering to myself, *I'm new at this. I must not say too much or too little. Hopefully, I can just follow Tig and the other constables' leads until I get a handle on how things are done here.*

The Sergeant offered me a seat in his small, cluttered office. It had sort of a musty, claustrophobic feel to it with files and boxes stacked everywhere. It sure didn't hold a candle to Corporal Todd's office back at the Moncton RCMP building.

The sergeant spent a few minutes while I listened intently to his instructions.

"Constable Mitchell, your trainer will be Senior Constable Melvin Silver. He'll oversee your ongoing training until you successfully complete the Recruit Field Training Program. He'll explain all of that when he comes in to work tomorrow."

I was eager to get going on the next step, so I continued to listen intently. I felt the sooner I began it the sooner I would become a real peace officer.

The Sergeant called to Tig and told him to show me around the general office. He was told to supply me with a key to the barracks where I could park my things and freshen up. We were both advised that coffee break was in twenty minutes at Bradford's Restaurant. The Sergeant was very clear to mention he wanted me to attend.

He only said, "I want you to meet some of the guys!"

Later, I would realize, no one missed the daily ritual of the morning coffee break at Bradford's. When all members finally arrived, the group numbered eleven. Throughout the coffee break, each member individually spoke with me. The whole thing felt choreographed. They each asked, in turn, a different topic question. I sensed that by the end of the session the group was able to form some opinion of how I'd perform as an RCMP member. The feeling I got from the group's general reaction was that it went well. At least that was how I felt when it was all over.

When I returned to the barracks, I felt somewhat exhausted. Between the long trip and the "hot seat" type interview, I was ready to lie down and close my eyes.

I only remember my last thoughts were, *Tomorrow will be easier. I'll get to sleep and make a fresh start in the morning.*

Bryce and Tig would go to bed much later. They must have been quiet when they came in because I never heard a sound all night until I awoke the next morning at 6:00 a.m. Tig and Calder seemed to be snoring in tandem.

I sarcastically thought, *now this should be a lot of fun—sleeping in this little bedroom with two guys that could snore the paint right off the walls. I guess I'll be buying another pillow so I can place it over my head every night to drown out the noise.*

I quietly got up and performed the normal bathroom activity. While I was washing up Tig turned over in his bed. My slight bit of noise must have awakened him.

I heard a groan. It was the type that one would make after being awakened from a hangover. To my surprise, I would later confirm that Tig had often over-indulged a bit too much during off-duty hours. He really liked his rye whisky, beer, and his Bacardi 1873 rum.

I ignored the groans, got dressed and went out to greet the day. I walked through the unlocked office door to meet with my trainer, Constable Mel Silver. We introduced ourselves and he indicated he had been working since 6:00 a.m. I acted quickly to let him know I was eager to start my Recruit Field Training. I asked if he could show me the binder and tell me what was expected. I wanted him to feel I was sincerely interested in the job.

I could tell he liked my attitude, so he proceeded to coach me through the process. Before the day was over, I had developed a great admiration for his mentoring technique. He was serious but relaxed and patient. He had an easy manner. That allowed us to talk about any facet of life or police work. I felt he was the first member other than Constable Grier that really influenced the image of what I wanted to become as a peace officer.

The days passed quickly as I tackled everything presented to me with the best of my ability. Before long, three weeks had elapsed. Mel advised he was going to recommend I be placed on the shift in a permanent position. This meant I would be able to work alone. I'm not saying three weeks was a long time, but I was eager and, in a hurry, to prove myself worthy of being a Mountie. It meant I wouldn't have to shadow another member like a dog on a leash.

I would be able to take my place as a regular member of the detachment on my own shift, albeit I was still on Recruit Field Training Program. There were a lot more testing hurdles to overcome before the six-month period would end. I was still on probation as a recruit until then.

Working with Mel had been very helpful. He had introduced me to most of the local townspeople; he showed me how to answer the phones; take complaints over the counter; make an arrest; and how to properly deliver a ticket. I assisted him twice while he arrested an impaired driver, so I was familiar with those procedures. He had monitored how I treated people very closely. Although it isn't much by today's standards, this was enough to get started in the1970s.

The rest was learned by reading policy and investigative practices. More importantly I gained practical experience by working with the other members and the public on a continuous basis. It was equally important to remember and to learn by my own mistakes.

CHAPTER 6

Hoodwinked

THE TIME HAD COME FOR me to work my very first evening shift. It ran from 6:00 p.m. to 2:00 a.m. The shift had been unusually quiet for such a clear night. One call for information had come in earlier, but nothing else. The last hour had been completely silent—no calls. I looked at my watch. It was close to 1:45 a.m. I had already checked all the doors of the several businesses in Vermilion without finding any problems. In total, I had checked four cars with varying numbers of occupants without finding anything unusual.

I wasn't really tired. Although I thought it was about time to return to the office to complete an action report for Sergeant Tibber and the dayshift members. It was a common practice performed by everyone on nightshift. It enabled pertinent information to be shared with the on-coming dayshift member(s). It allowed them to follow up any investigations, release prisoners, and be made aware of any intelligence information that may have been gathered during the previous shift. It also provided a written record of the shift's activities.

I started to head back to the office. I was about four blocks away when I noticed the taillights of a brown GMC pickup. I watched it intently for anything suspicious.

When it turned down a residential back alley driving very slowly, I said to myself, "Might as well check this one before I quit!"

It was a short distance from my location, so I caught up to it without any problem. As it continued to move slowly down the alley, I called Edmonton Telecoms to query the licence plates for wants or warrants. I engaged my emergency lights when I received a negative response. The truck stopped immediately.

Along with the feelings of excitement at the check, I experienced a certain amount of anxiousness. I have never been afraid of the dark, so I knew that wasn't it. I also knew it wasn't the traffic stop itself. I had stopped many vehicles during the day shifts with varying numbers of occupants without ever experiencing that feeling of uncertainty. During the GMC stop, it only lasted for several moments, but it still disturbed me at first. I later understood what had happened. It was the first time I had to face making all the decisions regarding that traffic stop, whereas the immediate support had always previously been there.

I'm talking about elements like maintaining control of the occupants; their safety; my safety; locating and dealing with the possible offence(s); writing up the paperwork correctly; and accepting the consequences for everything that I had said or the action I had taken during the transaction.

It was the first time I felt what it was like to be a peace officer working completely on his own.

It left me with an understanding of the depth of expertise required to successfully perform my duty as a peace officer. I had a lot to learn. The stillness of the night and the blackness of the sky reinforced that ominous feeling of uncertainty. I pushed through it by remembering that I chose this career, and it was my duty to perform it without fear or uncertainty and to be fair and to be just.

In an instant I reassured myself, *since most criminal activity occurred at night, I'd better get used to it. After all I was trained to perform such stops be it day or night—with support or without support!*

I slowly stepped out of the car. I stood for a moment, straining to see who was sitting in the vehicle with the aid of my high beam headlights. I saw two silhouettes as I approached from the rear left side, walking as close to the truck as possible. I stopped just short of the driver's door.

I was instructed to do that in training. It was recommended as the safest way to approach any vehicle stop. Standing to the side and behind the driver allowed me to see him, but without cranking his head uncomfortably to the left, he couldn't see me. I watched both occupants closely as the driver rolled his window down to greet me.

"What's the matter, Sir? I was just going home. We live three houses up there on the right."

"This is an Alberta Check Stop. I need to see your licence, registration, and insurance please."

He handed the required documents to me directly. It seemed he had them in hand before I even asked. It was almost like he expected to be stopped.

"Is this your truck? And has anyone been drinking tonight?"

He answered, "Yes, two whiskeys earlier at a friend's house party three miles north of town. My wife here is pregnant. She's in her seventh month. I just want to get her home. She's very tired."

As he spoke, I smelled the strong odour of liquor. I looked into his eyes while pointing my flashlight near his face. He didn't seem intoxicated.

"Where's the open liquor?"

Without hesitation, the man reached under the front centre seat of his truck and pulled out a part full bottle of Canadian Club Whiskey and placed it in the cup holder on his dash.

"I'll have to give you a ticket for that you know. So, give me a minute or two to write it up."

I returned to my vehicle with his particulars in my hand. I wanted to write the liquor charge up correctly so I could impress Mel. When I was partially finished with the ticket, I caught a glimpse of the passenger-side door opening. His wife was beginning to step out of the truck. I jumped out and walked up to her.

I stopped her and said, "Where are you going?"

She looked at me calmly, "I really don't feel well. Can I go home to lie down? It's just over there." She pointed to the back of a red trimmed house.

"Sure, you can. Do you need any help?"

She muttered a negative response. Then she somewhat waddled down the alley.

Not thinking too much about it, I returned to my car and finished the ticket.

I approached the driver once more. When I was just about to explain the ticket to the driver, I made a subconscious observation. The open bottle of whiskey was missing from the dash cup holder. I said, "Where's the Canadian Club bottle?"

The driver looked at me with a dumb grin then answered, "Sir, I don't know what you're talking about. What bottle?"

Right then, that feeling of when you screw up filled my chest. I wanted to get mad but couldn't. I knew it was my own fault. In training, they told us over and over, "Always seize the exhibit first, without it you have no evidence."

The guy was just playing the game. I searched the vehicle anyway but found nothing. I knew right then his wife had walked away with the open liquor. I had to let the man go. If I hadn't been standing in the complete darkness, he would have seen a Mountie with the "red face of embarrassment." I told no one at the detachment what had happened and dearly hoped that the guy wouldn't tell anyone either.

That's what I meant earlier about learning by my mistakes. The memory of the incident followed me relentlessly. I recalled it every time I dealt with an exhibit from that time onward. I never failed to seize the exhibit first at any other incident during the rest of my career.

CHAPTER 7

The Girl Next Door

WITHIN MY FIRST MONTH, an unusual chain of events happened. Four important incidents occurred one after the other. The first one involved the three of us living in the barracks. I explained how the barracks related to the layout of the detachment building system, but I left one important thing out.

In Vermilion, there was a door in the middle of our activity room that connected the sergeant's residence to the barracks. It was a locked door and the only one who had a key was the sergeant. He used the key at his whim. He entered anytime he wanted without regard for the time—night or day—or our privacy.

One of my first evenings after shift, Tig, Bryce, and I had just sat down after changing into civilian clothes. Bryce thought that it was time I was exposed to the finer points of having the odd drink of Bacardi's 1873 Rum. As a non-drinker, I wasn't too keen on the idea at first.

I agreed after thinking, *these guys are just trying to help me fit in, so one drink as friends can't hurt.* Bryce mixed me a rum and coke. I politely sipped it slowly while the conversation poured on.

I was suddenly curious. As I started to feel the effects of my first drink, I brought up the subject of the door. I asked Tig, 'What's the whole deal with the one-way access?"

"Tim, the one-key-entry thing is so Sergeant Tibber can wake one of us up when he receives a complaint after our normal working hours. You know that the latest anyone works is 2:00 a.m., and the dayshift doesn't normally come in until 8:00 a.m. So, sometimes serious matters come in during those off-hours."

That invited another question. "Yes, but how does he choose who goes to the complaint?"

"Well, normally whoever is on days off is left alone. One of the other two is sent to the complaint. That's why he has access to the barracks! If a complaint is serious enough, two of us might have to go. When one of us goes to a call after hours it's called voluntary overtime!" This brought up more questions for me. "What does that mean? We don't get paid for working during the middle of the night hours?"

Bryce was quick to respond in a loud voice, "You got it partner! We don't get paid!" He had had a lot more to drink than Tig and I had by that time.

It was plain to me even while slightly under the influence of that rum that Bryce had some dislike for voluntary overtime.

Tig suddenly interjected. "Look, we do get paid in a way! Say you attend a call after hours and it takes you four hours from the time you start the investigation until you return to the office. You get to record those hours. There's a book in the drawer under the front counter with 'Time in Lieu' written on the front. You'll find everyone's name in the book. Turn to your name and place the times you worked and the total number of hours it took to complete the investigation under the right columns. Time in Lieu means that you can get time off in lieu of being paid overtime."

"What good does putting it in the book do?" I asked.

"Well, when you get a significant amount of time built up, say forty-eight hours, then you can put in a leave pass for those hours. You get the sergeant or one of the corporals to sign it and you'll have that time off your regular shift if you want. Tim, it's not a bad deal."

As young men were inclined, we all overindulged a bit that night. On the upside, many more questions were answered for me during the process.

We had all agreed that the sergeant's continuous invasion into our private space was disruptive. Now, from my first week in Vermilion, the sergeant's sixteen-year-old daughter, Claudette, started entering our side from their side—also, at her whim.

It was kind of novel at first, we all laughed at it. It was very obvious to us; she was enamoured with someone. We each suspected that it was all of us at times. Fortunately, we knew she was only sixteen. We were very aware that nothing could come of her unsolicited flirtations. She was a very attractive girl with bright blue eyes, golden hair, and a body beyond her age. She was definitely off-limits.

Everything was going along fine until one evening the three of us had been sitting around talking when the sergeant's door opened. There stood Claudette. The sound of her light sensual voice was heard, "Hi, how are you boys tonight?"

We were so stunned no one said a word. We just stared at her. She was standing there in a see-through negligee with absolutely nothing under it. Her breasts and pubic area were in full view. If it had been her aim to get our attention, then she got our attention.

She stood motionless at the door for several moments. We all watched a strange redness fill her face. Realizing what was happening, she abruptly disappeared, effectively slamming the door shut.

I thought her father and mother must have been out for her to get away with those actions.

Bryce was first to speak, "What the hell was that? What a sleaze! This better not happen again!"

I wasn't sure if any of us were serious enough to take any action to stop her lewd behaviour. Even I knew it wouldn't be easy to explain her actions to Sergeant Tibber. The three of us were definitely heterosexual, and we normally really loved women. She was not a woman.

Tig was quick to remark, "She is just a girl! And a girl shouldn't look like that! A girl shouldn't be doing that!"

We were all upset, but no one could figure out how to tell the sergeant. He was strict and very conservative. We felt sure that he would rather believe it was our fault, and her actions were not his daughter's doing.

It was a dilemma that kept getting worse. She pulled semi-dressed stunts twice in the two weeks that followed. She had flashed in and out so fast we never had time to even yell at her.

Bryce had cornered her one day outside the office. She was walking back to her residence after visiting her dad. Bryce told us he had threatened to tell her father if she didn't stop.

He said, "She seems a bit scared, so I think she got the message?"

Several more weeks went by without incident. One Friday night a friend of Bryce's had slept over in the barracks after a late night of partying. He was an RCMP member like we were but posted at Slave Lake detachment.

About 6:30 a.m. Saturday morning we were all soundly sleeping. Claudette had seen fit to be more daring than usual. I didn't understand why she was doing it at that time. With more experience, I later came to realize many women have sexual fantasies that involved being naked in front of strangers and friends alike. I guess she was no different. At the time, we all felt she was a bit nuts.

We were all startled from our sleep by an unfamiliar yell by Bryce's friend, Lonnie. He had been sleeping on the sofa in the other room. Tig and I jumped up right away. We ran to the doorway of the activity room where we both stopped dead in our tracks. Claudette was standing with a t-shirt on and no bottoms at all. Lonnie was standing up naked, swearing at Claudette. He kept yelling at her to leave with the foulest of language. She looked like she was going to cry as she ran through the sergeant's door. Lonnie just stood there swearing with an obvious excited body part in full view. By that time, Bryce had gotten up. "What the hell happened here Lonnie? Why are you yelling? You'll wake up the sergeant! What's wrong?"

Lonnie suddenly realized that he was naked, so he grabbed his pants and put them on. He didn't answer Bryce right away.

"Well!" Bryce demanded.

Lonnie wiped his eyes to completely wake up. "Bryce, I was completely asleep when I began to have a dream. It seemed so real that it woke me up. When I opened my eyes, I saw the sergeant's daughter, Claudette, standing over me, and she had her hand on my thing. Sorry I overreacted, but this makes me angry. I didn't do anything to her. It isn't my fault. I don't want to get charged for anything. She's only sixteen! Right?"

Lonnie went on and on until he got it out of his system. Bryce was adamant that we'd have to talk to Sergeant Tibber that morning. He went back into the bedroom to get dressed and prepared for what was to come.

Lonnie wanted nothing to do with it. He got dressed, and without even saying good-bye got into his car and left. I never saw him again. Unfortunately, he was the member who got murdered in Mexico that same year under suspicious circumstances.

While we all took our turns in the shower, I couldn't help but think, *The stuff is really going to hit the fan today! It should be interesting. Hopefully, the sergeant will take the news all right?*

I finished getting ready then headed down to Chan's Restaurant for breakfast with Tig and Bryce. We sat and discussed how to deal with the matter. Who would confront the sergeant? Finally, Bryce agreed he'd be the one to break the news to Sergeant Tibber.

A feeling of uncertainty permeated the office that morning. As time elapsed, Bryce continued to hold back. Tig and I were getting anxious, so we approached him, "What's going on? Are we going to talk to him or not?" Tig asked insistently. I stood there silently waiting for Bryce to answer him. I was still very new to the Force. That fact made me keenly interested in witnessing how an incident like that was handled.

A few minutes went by before Bryce answered, "Okay, I'll see him now! You two come with me in case I need back-up."

Tig and I stood at the sergeant's office doorway and listened while Bryce got the boss's attention. I don't remember his exact words, but Bryce provided the sergeant with a vivid picture of what had been happening. He did it in the most subtle and polite way. I was amazed at the effect it had on Sergeant Tibber. His ears and face got red, then almost crimson, as Bryce finished the tale. The sergeant sat in silence. For a time, we didn't know what to expect. It left us feeling that it could go either way. Before he gave his reply, it was like we were in a perpetual limbo. It was like taking part in a contest to see who could hold his breath the longest before fainting.

Finally, the sergeant spoke, "I'm very sorry you all had to witness that! I want to thank you for being gentlemen." His voice cracked—stopped— then carried on, "I promise that it will never happen again! Can I count on you to let it die here and now? He took a breath then stopped talking.

A unanimous, "Yes, Sergeant Tibber!" was heard from the tattling three. Surprisingly, he seemed to be genuinely humbled by the whole affair. He wasn't one to normally apologize for anything.

After we had met for coffee at Chan's Bryce said, "That should be the end of it. So, let's forget it and never bring it up again."

Tig and I nodded in agreement.

The Hitchhiker

THE FIRST THREE MONTHS HAD been very eventful for me. It was like incident after incident happened in quick succession. Whenever I worked alone something different challenged me, leaving me with new knowledge of how to handle myself.

One morning, when I had spoken with Mel about my Recruit Field Training Handbook, one of the corporals interrupted, "Can Tim take a highway patrol position today? I have no one to cover, and Bryce is away at court."

Mel looked at me as if it was my decision alone. I quickly said "Sure, if it's okay Mel, I'll do it!" He approved, so I grabbed the keys and proceeded to pick up my briefcase, ticket book, and flashlight. Off I went with a smile of excitement on my face. Highway Patrol Duties would be a completely new duty for me. I had worked as a ride-a-long member with Bryce a couple of times, so I had some experience. I certainly felt ready and qualified. I had just completed a radar course the week before.

But once I started, I found the first couple of ticket deliveries a bit shaky. It took several times to get into a comfortable routine. I made sure to adhere to all the proper practices I had learned on the radar course. I wanted to do everything just right.

The shift went on; ticket after ticket was delivered until I had become very comfortable. During that one shift, I had dealt with several denials and excuses for speeding. I began to enjoy the cat and mouse game that occurred between officer and violator. I found the emotional combat, the continuous potential danger, and the rare, pleasant interaction surprisingly invigorating.

Many times, that day I thought, *I love this job, it has the 'wow factor' for me!* When I walked into the office with a fist full of tickets both Mel and the corporal l were impressed.

The Corporal spoke up before I even had a chance to sit down, "Considering you've done such a great job, would you like to fill in again tomorrow?"

I looked at Mel. He could see I wanted to, so the deal was made. The next day, I would be a highway patrolman again. I was happy. I loved the many facets of police work. I kept thinking, *every day something new would happen!* The last thing on my mind was considering the negative side. I'm referring to potential injury that could occur if I made any mistakes.

The next shift came quickly. I was eagerly patrolling the highway enjoying the enforcement role. I hadn't known that during the night we had experienced a drop in temperature causing some areas of black ice on the edges of the highway. I was unfamiliar with the consequences of that roadway condition. I was even unaware of its appearance. Although there were areas of intermittent blowing snow, the highway looked safe and fairly dry to me.

About two hours into the shift, I observed a hitchhiker walking on the wrong side of the road with the flow of traffic. In Alberta, it was illegal to do so although we very rarely charged anyone for that offence. Instead, we used it as grounds to check hitchhikers to ascertain if they were just good people travelling from place to place or criminals committing crimes while on their journey.

I drove up to the male hitchhiker's location. I got out of the car and observed a male about twenty, with a shaved head, a thin winter jacket, and a small backpack. He was polite and co-operative as we talked. I noticed that he was shivering a bit, so I asked him, "Would you like to have a seat in the car to stay warm while I run your name?"

"Sure, sir!" He started to open the back door when I stopped him. I felt he was not a threat.

"Hop into the front, it's okay." While awaiting the results of his name query, I asked several more questions. His candid answers and general demeanour confirmed to me he was a good guy. Very shortly, Edmonton Telecoms confirmed that he had no wants or warrants.

I couldn't help but feel sorry for the guy having to hitchhike in the cold. I offered to drive him as far as Mannville, the next closest town to Edmonton, which was his intended destination. He seemed grateful for that suggestion, so off we went. The miles quickly whistled by as I drove a bit faster than normal. We continued our friendly conversation.

I realized we were getting close to Mannville so I began to slow down. About halfway through a right-hand curve my front tire caught a patch of black ice. Suddenly the vehicle went out of control. I frantically manoeuvred the steering wheel to counteract the spin. I used every bit of driver training experience the Force had given me to reclaim control of the car. I remember watching helplessly as signs, fence posts, and light poles streaked past the windows of my car. At one point. all I could do was hang on to the steering wheel and wait for the inevitable.

I was sure that we would hear the crash of impact at any moment, so I braced myself and remember yelling, "Hang on!" to the hitchhiker.

As suddenly as it started it was all over. I found myself unhurt. My vehicle was sitting in the middle of the proper lane and pointing in the correct direction. The hitchhiker and I instinctively looked at each other. I felt a little shaken. The hitchhiker's face was very pale. He was sitting slightly bent forward with both hands literally gripping the dash. For a time, we sat there, speechless without making a move.

He was the first one to speak, "Damn you guys can drive! To recover from that was impossible! It must be some driving course that they teach you in Regina!"

I said nothing. I let my foot off the brake and proceeded down the road. After a short distance, I returned to the conversation with him.

"I agree the Force did provide us with a great driving course, but I can't take credit as luck had a lot to do with the outcome." I tried to be humble.

The hitchhiker refused to believe that luck had anything to do with it. At the drop-off destination, he thanked me again and praised me for the stupendous driving. With my windows still down, I began to turn around to return to the Vermilion area. I heard him say, "Man, you guys can drive!" I waved at him and drove on.

Little did the hitchhiker know it was an entity greater than I that had saved us! I never spoke of the event for years. It was not until time and space completely separated me from the Vermilion posting did I recount the incident. To this day, I shudder to think what could have happened to either of us physically or to my career if things had turned out differently.

CHAPTER 9

My First Subpoena

WITH THE BLACK ICE INCIDENT behind me, warmer days finally arrived. It was a dry spring with a lot of sun. That kind of weather was a welcomed change to my first couple of months in Vermilion. My experience and training had been ongoing. I began to feel very at ease with the job. I was sure enough to handle most calls but smart enough to ask for guidance when it was appropriate.

Mysteriously, I had overlooked the service of subpoena. It was one of the things I had to check off in my recruit field training book. The list of things to do seemed endless. I began to feel it wasn't going to end, so I approached Mel to see if any subpoenas had to be served.

Corporal Butler was sitting within earshot of my conversation. He was a strict and unforgiving man. Instead of just asking, he routinely gave orders. In a superior tone he interrupted us, "So you want to serve a subpoena, do you Constable Mitchell?"

Mel jumped in, "Have you got one Corporal Butler? If so, I'll take it, Tim can probably do it for you!" I knew Mel didn't like the corporal very much. I didn't realize it at the time, but he jumped in to protect me like a brother would have done. It was plain to me that Mel and the Corporal seemed to be opposites.

"Can't Constable Mitchell speak for himself?"

I answered before Mel could reply, "Yes, I can Corporal! If you have one, I'll be glad to serve it for you."

I couldn't believe it when I saw Corporal Butler return a snake-like smile. I walked toward him and took the subpoena. It was to be delivered to a farm location about five miles out of town. Mel helped me look up the location on the area map in the sergeant's office. It looked like a straightforward job to me.

I loaded up a rural car with the subpoena in my briefcase. I headed out on Highway #42. It didn't take long to find the address. I turned into the farmyard right away. Before coming to a complete stop near the house, I slowly drove past the open barn, and I didn't spot anyone working as I passed it. Everything seemed quiet and fine. The farm appeared to be abandoned. I couldn't see anyone around at all.

I was born left-handed, but growing up in the 1950s, schoolteachers made lefties like me change hands. So, I wrote right-handed, but my strongest preferred hand was still my left hand. In 1975 it was also too early for the Force to accept such a condition for its candidates, so I carried my gun on the right.

Luckily, I was trained to shoot proficiently with both hands. Up to then I had never guessed it would be a good thing the Force trained me that way.

When I stopped the car, I picked up the subpoena and began to open my door. Before I could exit, I suddenly found myself on the ground. I was lying on my left side with my left arm extended outward and over my head. My face was about three inches from the dirt. I felt a severe pain in my left hand. Because of my position, I couldn't move. My left leg was on the ground partially under my car and my right leg was still hung up in the car. A sense of panic set in. I struggled to move or roll away from the pain. It just got worse by the second. I arched my back and twisted my head where it wouldn't naturally go. I caught a glimpse of a German shepherd that was trying to tear my hand off. I reached with my right hand into my holster.

Without being able to see the dog completely, I pointed in the general direction and fired, and fired, and fired until all I heard was the clicking sound. It was the sound of the firing pin re-striking the expended rounds for the second time. I shook, and then stopped pulling the trigger, dropping my gun in the dirt in the process.

The pain was still there but the pulling had ceased. I was stunned, but in a frantic effort I twisted and pulled until I was able to get free of the car. This allowed me to roll onto my stomach and pull myself to a half sitting position. The vision of the dead dog with my hand still in its mouth was to be short-lived. I quickly pulled my hand out somehow. I lifted it towards my face and watched in horror at the amount of blood spewing from my palm.

I stood up, still a bit dazed and angry. *There had been no sound, no indication, how could I have been caught off-guard like that? Damn dog*!

I looked up and there stood the dog's owner. He was pale and about to speak. I stopped him by responding to the attack with angry words. I know now it was the adrenaline speaking. I can't remember exactly what I said. But yelling, some swearing, and threats of a lawsuit were all part of my reaction.

He had no reply. He just stood there. I wrapped my bleeding hand with pieces of paper towel I got from my car. I had placed a roll of it on the front seat to wipe the dust from my shiny boots. I wanted to keep them looking professional.

I glared at the man as I backed up the car. I drove out of the yard watching him in my rear-view mirror. My hand throbbed with pain. I looked down at it just as I turned onto the highway. The blood had seeped through the paper towels. It was soaking my left pant leg and dripping onto the floor. Without another thought I drove directly to the Vermilion hospital.

To my surprise, the doctors just gave me a tetanus shot and bandaged it. I hadn't needed stitches, or a rabies shot. I was grateful for the prompt service, so I thanked the doctor and shook his hand. He indicated for me to be sure to keep the still throbbing left hand elevated against my chest.

It was time to return to the office to face the consequences. I was fairly certain the dog's owner would have made a complaint by then. I walked directly into the sergeant's office sporting my bandaged hand. He could plainly see the dirt on my uniform shirt and pants. Sergeant Tibber looked at me dumbfounded. "What happened? Are you alright?" He stood up from his desk and walked closer to me as if he wanted to help.

"I'll be fine, Sir. I came in to tell you to expect a complaint. Can I sit down? My hand still hurts! So, I can tell you the whole story." The sergeant listened intently as I graphically explained my every move—even the parts of me swearing at the owner. He remained quiet through the whole story.

When I was finished, I bent my head down in shame. While waiting for his reaction, I thought, *I'm in big trouble now. I might as well pack my bags and go home.*

Sergeant Tibber looked at me and said, "What did the doctor say about your hand? Will you have any permanent damage to it?"

His unexpected concern caught me off guard. I stammered a little before I answered, "No, it'll be fine; he told me I should be fine in a week or so."

"Don't worry Tim. I'll take care of the dog's owner. I know him; there won't be any trouble. And don't worry about not serving the subpoena; I'll serve it when I call him into the office."

I was relieved that Sergeant Tibber showed me such compassion. I had never seen that side of him before. His immediate defensive position in my favour impressed me. I really appreciated his belief in my version of the incident. It struck a chord within me that I have never forgotten.

What Sheep?

I WAS PLACED ON LIGHT duties for the next four shifts. I stayed in the office taking complaints by phone and assisted with front counter duties. By the Tuesday of the next week, I felt much better. After getting a report from the doctor, the sergeant saw fit to put me back on full duty.

Everyone had been told the dog story, including Tig and Bryce. They treated me differently after that. I think it was with more respect. Their attitudes had left me with a real sense of belonging to the detachment and to the Force. For the short term at least, I floated along with a feeling of satisfaction and fulfilment.

Then I realized I still had to serve a subpoena. As relentless as the sunrise, I did my best to put the unfortunate dog incident behind me. I was more than aware I was at the beginning of my career.

"I would surely have to face a lot more than a bite from a dog," I said to myself.

I decided instead of waiting to be given another subpoena, I would approach Mel to ask for several of them to serve. That way I would put the uneasy feelings brought about by the dog bite far behind me.

He seemed pleasantly surprised. Without saying a word, he reached into his briefcase and pulled out four of them. Three subpoenas were to be served in town, but one was a rural address out in the same area as the first subpoena. "Tim, are you sure you're up for this?"

Deep down I was still a little spooked by the dog bite, but I answered Mel with confidence anyway.

"Of course, Mel! I'll be careful unless you want to come with me?" I joked.

He had to joke back, "To be safe, do you want to take the detachment shot gun with you just in case?"

I laughed but didn't answer. I proceeded to pack up my police vehicle. I drove around town to serve the municipal subpoenas first. I had no problem finding the appropriate addresses and the exact recipients. By the third subpoena I began to believe, *this duty was a piece of cake!* Now it was time to serve that last subpoena. I had already checked the farm location on the map. It was back out in the same area as before. With the last rural incident still fresh in my mind I was determined to be more cautious.

I remember distinctly thinking, and most likely speaking it out loud to myself, "if something were to happen again, well I don't know what the sergeant would do?" I remained a bit nervous. *Would they ever let me work alone again?* I wrestled a little with those thoughts as I got closer to my intended destination.

Very soon I found the address. I could see the house from the road. It was elevated several metres above the rest of the property. For the most part, the farmyard was absent of trees.

I drove in slowly, swivelling my head back and forth, anxiously looking for any signs of trouble. Like the other place, everything seemed quiet. I took the precaution of even phoning the residence before leaving the office. The owner was very polite and co-operative. He was expecting me, so I felt assured there would be no trouble. I pulled up to the front of the green bungalow then turned off my ignition. I looked down at the subpoena to review what I had to say.

While casually looking down at the paperwork, I felt a sudden jolt and heard a loud crash. Something had hit the left rear of my car. At first, I thought it was another vehicle. I cranked my head to the left and couldn't believe my eyes. "Not again?" I yelled. Before I could react, I felt another sudden jolt with a loud crash. I turned completely in the seat. I saw the biggest sheep, ram, or goat, whatever it was, try to strike my car for a third time. The monster stood at least five feet at its shoulders. He bent his head down for another strike when a slender man appeared. I watched as he quickly chased the creature off with a stick.

The unexpected happened for the second time, *who's going to believe this one?* I was bewildered. *What was I supposed to tell the sergeant this time? What kind of place is Vermilion anyway?* So many thoughts rushed at me all at once.

The man saw that I wasn't making a move to get out of my car. He slowly opened my door and said, "Everything is fine now. I'm so sorry about your car. I forgot to tie Allistair up. He's our 'attack ram.' He rams everything that comes into the yard."

By the time I stepped out of the car to survey the damage I was able to act as if I was under control. I looked at three large caved in areas. I looked around to see where the ram had gone while the owner kept talking.

"It's totally my fault, Sir! Just have your sergeant send me the bill—I'll take care of it."

He stuck out his hand to greet me as the owner of the farm. I was able to confirm his was the name on the subpoena.

After the ram was properly secured, we spent about a half an hour together having coffee in his residence. I found him to be a nice guy. During the conversation, I related the dog story of the week before to him. I thought he might have laughed a bit, but instead, he seemed genuinely concerned over the incident. I thanked him for his hospitality then left after shaking his hand once more.

The damage to the police car and the "ramming" had been another unique experience for me. Unfortunately, I still had one problem; What were they going to say back at the detachment?

I quickly drove the dented police car back to the office parking lot. I knew I had to tell the sergeant about yet another stupid incident. I walked across the office floor to Tibber's office. It was déjà vu, just like the previous week. He looked up from his paperwork asking the definitive question, "Well Tim, how did it go this time?"

In that second before answering the sergeant, the incident played through my head. I found the whole thing funny. I smiled and almost chuckled as I sat down to explain. I felt like beginning the story with "Once upon a time there was a young Mountie..." but stopped short of that.

Once the ordeal was fully explained, Sergeant Tibber laughed out loud. He kept on laughing, even when he spoke, "Tim! If you had any luck at all it would be bad luck!"

I found myself laughing along with him because it was funny. I could see myself—a pale little RCMP member hanging on to his steering wheel for comfort while an "attack ram" dented the heck out of his car.

I secretly thought, *yeah! They'll be laughing about this for a long time, I'd better get used to it.*

CHAPTER 11

The Waterfall

THE POLICE CAR GOT FIXED and the man paid for the damages as promised. The work went on. Every interaction with other members and the public developed more confidence. By my fifth month in Vermilion, I had made several friends outside the Force. I knew all the business owners, the bank employees, and most of the local people around town. I made every attempt to be fair, honest, and most of all, friendly.

It became routine for any one of the townspeople to approach me, especially while I was alone having coffee at Chan's Restaurant. By that time, they readily provided me with important rumours and intelligence regarding crime activity in the area. I was supplied with suspect names concerning some specific thefts and break-ins. At first, I shared the information with Tig and Bryce, as I didn't know quite how to handle it. After completing several cases preparing warrants and dealing with arresting the local criminals, I started working independently. It was a far cry from writing a speeding or a liquor ticket.

The Vermilion experience gave me much more: the value of honesty, the need for compassion, and what I call a "third eye." I can only describe it as a strange phenomenon that I experienced. It seemed to make it easier for me to determine fact from fiction. It also included a newfound ability to sense when something was about to go wrong slightly before it happened. I always presumed it was a result of gaining experience as a peace officer. I've talked about it to others throughout my career, but they have all laughed or just outright denied the possibility of its existence.

After a while I never brought it up again. But that didn't stop me from continuing to use it. I looked at it as my own personal safety tool.

Vermilion was a grand place to learn. Most of all, it gave me the confidence to stand up for what I believed to be right regardless of the consequences. What follows is an example of the type of incident I mean.

The evening shift consisted of three members: Corporal Butler and a constable on rural duties, while I was scheduled to work the municipal shift.

At about 2:15 a.m. things were going along fine until a call came into the office from Edmonton Telecoms. The dispatcher explained an anonymous report was received indicating a residence had been broken into. Information suggested someone was still prowling around inside.

I had never attended an actual break-in in progress before, so I wanted to consult Corporal Butler. I approached his office. I saw that he was lecturing and yelling at the other constable. I waited for a break in the conversation and then interrupted him. I told Corporal Butler about the complaint. He seemed annoyed that I even mentioned it. "You go ahead. You can handle it! Call if you need assistance!" Without taking a breath, he turned his head back to the other constable and carried on with his argument. It appeared I was on my own.

I found the address on the map; it was only a few streets away from the detachment. While en route, I tried to anticipate all the possible scenarios that might occur when I arrived. Within four minutes I was sitting in my car in front of the residence. I noticed every light in the two-story older home was on. I stared through my side window and windshield at a strange sight. I could see water running down every wall and down every light fixture.

I was amazed because I knew the danger of mixing water and electricity.

"Why aren't the lights being shorted out?" I said aloud to myself. It seemed very odd to me at the time.

I contacted Edmonton Telecoms as per procedure. I stated my location and indicated I would be out of radio contact for several minutes to investigate. I didn't have a portable radio with me on that occasion so I couldn't maintain contact. I really didn't have a clue what to expect. I made a final decision after some thought about the pros and cons of my predicament. The safest thing to do was to leave my police car unlocked and running. I believed my chances to get help would be improved, especially if I got hurt and had to limp or crawl back. The town had always rolled up its sidewalks by that time of night. I saw no one about so leaving the car running was a safe bet to take.

I exited the car for a closer look. I peered into every window. The results were the same. I saw water running down the walls and down the light fixtures. Water was even running down the second-floor steps. It looked like a cascading waterfall. It was something you would only expect to see in the movies.

I diligently surveyed the area but couldn't see anyone moving around inside. I approached the front door. My first thought was, *this may be a set up or an ambush for the police, so I must be careful.* Alternately I thought, *someone may be hurt inside. If I don't hurry, they might die. Whatever this is I must go in.*

I twisted the front entrance door handle. It was unlocked. While standing to one side, I swung it open. The running water made a hollow eerie sound as it ran through the house.

I yelled into the residence, "Is anybody in here? It's the police! Do you need assistance?" I waited and listened. There was no answer.

I stepped inside, straining my ears to detect any signs of activity. All I could hear was the repetitive sloshing noise of my own boots as I walked across the floor. With my flashlight in one hand, I carefully checked every room on the main floor. I found no one. I remained on-guard of my surroundings; I expected to see someone jump out at me at any time. The lights in the house began to flicker intermittently.

I remember thinking, *Lights don't fail me now! Stay on just a little longer*! I had forgotten to put new batteries in my flashlight, so I knew it was very dim. I remember that I mumbled to myself, *if it turns black in here, I'll not be able to finish my search.*

It was time to climb the waterfall to find its source. I reached the top of the staircase but not without almost slipping twice on the wet uneven steps. I looked back at the image below in amazement. It was the most unique view that I had ever seen in my life. It was truly a rushing bubbling waterfall running down the steps.

Once again, I called out, "Is anybody here! This is the police! Do you need help?" I heard a groaning sound of someone in pain. I followed the sounds directly to the ensuite bathroom. A young man clothed only in short underwear came into view. He was shivering, sitting on the floor with his head down. He looked as if he was drunk or drugged up. Close to his hand, I spotted a copper pipe sticking out of the wall spewing water onto the floor.

As I got closer, he moaned again. I saw definite signs of blood. A diluted mixture of blood and fresh water had filled the displaced sink on the floor. The colour red seemed everywhere. Areas of dried clotted blood were stuck to the inside of his forearms. I took a minute to turn off the valve on the wall just below the broken copper pipe.

I placed my hand on his shoulder and asked, "Are you alright? What happened?"

As he tried to answer, I visually examined him further and confirmed that the cuts had stopped bleeding. I couldn't find any other injuries. While continuing to talk with him, I gradually was able to stand him up. The more questions I asked the more he seemed to recover.

He was able to reveal his name was Greg and that he was sixteen. He said that he was partying with two friends earlier while drinking and dropping acid. He didn't remember breaking off the sink but recalled being very thirsty. I also determined that he lived there as it was his father's house.

"Where are your friends now?"

He answered in a very low tone coupled with hard-to-understand slurred speech. Nevertheless, I was able to piece enough together to get that his friends had left some time ago.

"Greg, who broke the sink off?"

He replied, "I don... don't know, I cud'hent ge... het the waa... terr out!"

I assumed that it was not a break-in if he lived at the residence. I felt that Greg most likely broke off the sink himself. With my present information, I didn't think I would be able to prove otherwise. Later, I found out his parents had left him while they visited a sick grandmother in Edmonton. His two friends were well known to us as "trouble." I knew then they would have to be interviewed to complete the investigation.

Greg put on the long coat I found in a nearby closet. I wanted to keep him as warm as possible to reduce any shock. I steadied him as we climbed down the stairs to the main floor. Within moments, we found ourselves outside, closing the front door to the residence.

It is time to get this kid checked out at the hospital, I thought. I turned to direct him towards my car when I noticed Corporal Butler standing at my vehicle. I approached the corporal and briefly related what had transpired. I indicated that I was taking Greg to the hospital to get examined before investigating any further.

He just glared at me. Then he officiously answered, "Yes, and when you're finished, I'd like to see you about a matter." His curt reaction threw me off a little, but I remained focused on the case at hand. I shrugged it off as it just being his normal demeanour.

The whole ordeal had taken about three hours. That included the initial search and recovery of the youth at the house, the examination at the hospital, and finally, the verification of Greg's story after interviewing his two friends. It wasn't until then that I released him into an uncle's custody. I had determined that Greg's story was accurate. The other two youths had watched Greg break off the sink. They got scared because of the blood and left the house without him.

After another half hour of report writing, the paperwork had been completed. I proudly placed the concluded file on Corporal Butler's desk for review. The case had been completed successfully. Tired and utterly exhausted, the stress of the long shift had weighed heavily on me. I was looking forward to a good sleep.

I was about to head into the barracks when Corporal Butler's last words suddenly rang in my head—I sat back down awaiting his return to the office. I couldn't help but wonder why he wanted to talk to me. It a few short minutes I was going to find out what his stress was all about.

CHAPTER 12

The Litmus Test

JUST BEFORE NODDING OFF AT my workstation desk, Corporal Butler walked in. He looked directly at me then pointed to his office. I instinctively followed him then sat down. He had a serious, angry look on his face.

I shuddered a little from feeling cold then yawned as I was over-tired. His pointing action had given me thoughts that drained me even more.

I waited as patiently as I could. Not saying a word out loud hadn't stopped my mind from asking those ominous questions.

Will this shift never come to an end? What did I do that was so wrong? I just want to go to sleep!

Corporal Butler started talking. "I need you to answer some very important questions that I have about your lackadaisical approach to this case."

"Is there a problem with what I did in the house or with the suspect corporal?"

A quick, almost angry response was catapulted back to me. "Yes, several problems, but one in particular that disturbs me! One that might land you in Service Court! So be sure to think before you answer it!'

I was dumbfounded. *What was with his angry attitude?* I bit my tongue and decided to remain silent and just listen. I racked my brains, but I couldn't come up any reasons why I was in trouble. *What had I done so horribly wrong?*

I was so tired that I still can't remember if I spoke those words out loud, or just thought of them.

I took a gulp of air to shake off my tiredness. Within the next few moments, I remembered when I first saw Corporal Butler.

It was just after I had closed the front door to the flooded residence. He was standing against my police car's driver side door with his arms folded in that superior manner he had. With that vision, I quickly reviewed the complete incident.

The rear door to my car was locked when I tried to place Greg in the back seat for transport to the hospital. I struggled to justify why I hadn't thought of it before. In my defence, I guessed I had been too concerned about taking care of the injured Greg to think of much else.

It was then that Corporal Butler jingled the keys in his right hand. Accompanied with this familiar snake-like grin he presented them to me.

I took a silent wild guess, "This whole thing must be the unlocked police car I had left running?"

I looked directly at Corporal Butler.

"I think I acted with common sense. I left the car unlocked because I had no assistance; no portable radio, or not enough information to know whether it was a set-up to injure the police. I didn't even know if it was an actual break and enter in progress—or someone injured inside who needed assistance. My actions were based on my own safety and the victim's safety."

I hesitated to take a breath. I began to continue, but Corporal Butler abruptly cut me off. He returned to the same accusations as if he hadn't heard my previous explanation.

"What I want you to answer, first, is why your police car was left running and unlocked? You were in there more than twenty minutes?

Why didn't you call Edmonton Telecoms with your portable radio to update your status? These are all Service Court offences. Be prepared to face the allegations of misconduct!"

I started to defend my actions again, but he yelled his response.

"Don't interrupt me and don't answer now! I'll give you the rest of the night to think about it. Be here promptly at 8:00 a.m. for a hearing. Do you understand?

To make my uncertainty worse, I knew very little of Force Policies and Service Court. I later realized that to have knowledge of such matters was like being armed with an invisible shield. Armour I would gain in my later service that would prevent this anguish from ever happening again.

Service Court was the Force equivalent to a Judicial Court made up of members of the RCMP organization. It normally dealt with issues like dress, deportment, conduct, and failure to comply with procedures. A member found guilty in Service Court could suffer a sentence varying from a fine in some form to a recommendation for dismissal. It wasn't to be taken lightly.

I kept thinking, *this is ridiculous, being accused of misconduct! Doesn't Corporal Butler understand? All I did was to help someone. Wasn't the case handled without incident? I see no sense in it.*

With all that had happened in the five months I was posted in Vermilion, the situation seemed to be the worst. I sat there quietly feeling my career was in serious trouble, maybe over altogether. I hadn't even finished my six-month probation or finished my recruit field training.

He continued to speak, "You need to get prepared for the hearing. I'd suggest if you're wise, you'll get some informed advice before 8:00 a.am! Good night! I'm off shift."

Corporal Butler's rapid delivery of each remark made my headache. After that mouthful, I really disliked him. I gave him a nod to indicate that I understood. Without further hesitation, he left the room and walked out of the office.

Following a couple of hard swallows, I asked myself, "What will I do? I am so tired and it's past 4:00 a.m. I must be here in less than four hours. I don't have much time to prepare a defence for all of this! I don't even know where to start?"

I had been up for almost twenty-four hours by then. I realized there would be no rest until the situation was resolved. I made some coffee while pondering my defence. There was a part of me that still refused to believe my predicament. I had to get help. I hated to wake up Mel, but he was all I had for support. He was my trainer. On several occasions, he had been clear about his role as my trainer. I could consult with him at any time. I hesitantly picked up the phone and dialled his number.

In no time my "Zero Hour," 8:00 a.m., had arrived. I found myself in the main office. Corporal Butler had seated me on a single chair in front of the mock judges; Sergeant Tibber, the other corporal, and himself. Mel was positioned a short distance behind me waiting for the proceedings to begin. I sat on the edge of my seat in anticipation. The fact that I had a capable mentor supporting me helped a great deal. Three other constables, including Tig and Bryce, were also present. I hadn't been able to speak to them earlier. I saw Tig mouth the words, "It'll be okay," from across the room.

To save time and to skip all the banter that came into play during the mock trial, I would like to paraphrase what occurred next.

Corporal Butler, in his officious manner, stated the charges, then asked me the same questions publicly that he had privately attacked me with at 4:00 a.m. Namely, why had I left my police car unattended, running, and unlocked. Then he repeated the additional act of failing to notify Edmonton Telecoms of my status within the allotted time. As if this wasn't enough, he added a final twist. Because of my unknown status, he alleged members had to be called from other duties to assist. Of course, he was referring to the other constable and himself that were sitting at the office on duty. He further alleged that my actions could have placed the assisting members in danger, because I failed to share the nature of the complaint prior to their arrival.

To a civilian onlooker, and indeed, to me, these allegations sounded dire. I sat there contemplating how to give a correct response. Before I could say anything, Mel spoke up. He insisted that I could justify my actions. He eloquently stated I acted using a process of common sense while considering the safety of the injured young man and myself.

Suddenly all eyes were on me. It was my turn.

A combination of anger and fear gripped my chest. I took a deep breath hoping to expel just the fear. I remained silent as Sergeant Tibber requested an answer to the questions. I was to start with the unlocked police vehicle allegation. I looked around the room. All I could see were solemn faces staring back at me. Each one of them seemed to be holding their breath in anticipation of my justification. In that moment, I felt alone standing against them all.

I began by going through my on-scene thought process, explaining how I considered the possible scenarios that might happen when I entered the residence. I expressed my reasoning for leaving the vehicle unlocked and running by stressing the safety factors involved. I ensured that the sergeant knew that I couldn't leave the injured youth and contact Edmonton Telecoms at the same time.

I had no portable radio that shift. I pointed to the top of the bookcase where three radios were being charged. I explained, "The unserviceable one with the red sticker was the only one left when I came on duty. Corporal Butler and the rural constable had the other two radios."

I advised the judges that I tried the radio to be sure and confirmed it wasn't working. I testified that I had informed Corporal Butler at the beginning of my shift of the radio situation.

He responded by saying, "Make do!"

I took another breath then continued. "As far as the contact with Telecoms, I did inform Edmonton that I'd be at the scene and out of radio contact. I took approximately twenty-two minutes before I was able to walk out of the front door with the youth."

I hesitated for a moment to determine if I had answered all the questions completely. Then it struck me. I hadn't answered the question about advising Corporal Butler of the case particulars.

Before anyone could respond I continued, "I had given Corporal Butler all the complaint particulars, especially the address, when I informed him, I didn't have a portable radio. That was when he told me to make do!"

I remember that my voice was a little shaky during some of the testimony, but I answered as professionally as I could.

Sergeant Tibber turned directly to Corporal Butler with a strange look. After a few moments of silence, he made a statement of his findings directly and plainly. He alternately switched his looks back and forth from me to Corporal Butler.

"I find that the allegations are completely unfounded! I also find that, although it's unusual to leave a police vehicle running and insecure, in this case I find it was completely justified!"

Corporal Butler turned slightly red. It appeared that he wasn't going to take the embarrassing loss very well. In that moment, I had gotten the feeling that someone would have to pay for the sergeant's decision. I was sure that someone would be me.

I sat there motionless. I couldn't believe it was over. The weight of a thousand elephants fell off my back. I watched as the whole office seemed to breathe a sigh of relief. Corporal Butler, Sergeant Tibber, and the rest of the members and staff arrived at my seated location almost simultaneously. They were all laughing and smiling. Each NCO took his turn shaking my hand.

I suddenly clued into what had just happened to me. This had been a test of my character and my ability to act under stressful circumstances. Butler had been acting right up to his red face. He laughed as he congratulated me on holding up, stating, "You will be experiencing a lot more than that throughout your career, especially if you continue to make the right decision for the right reasons. It's part of the life! You did fine, Constable Mitchell!"

I sat there totally speechless for what seemed forever. I almost felt embarrassed that I hadn't seen it coming. Being extremely tired and slightly overwhelmed, all I could do was smile and nod my head in acknowledgement for the office support.

I gave Mel special thanks. He insisted that it wasn't necessary. He said they had been waiting a week or two for the right scenario to invoke the Service Court experience for me.

The survival of that exercise had broadened my scope of understanding of the life I could expect with the Force. The first few months of training in the field does jar the new member into a "reality check." Questions raced through my mind: *Is this the proper career choice for me? Can I handle the job? Do I have realistic expectations? Am I suited for this work* These were things that only I could answer.

The vision I saw was one of a hard road to travel. It would be one of constant testing of one's confidence. It would be a career fraught with overwhelming obstacles tempered with exciting triumphs. It would become a life I would grow to love.

CHAPTER 13

The Pick-Up Complaint

DURING MY TIME IN VERMILION, I had gone out with at least seven women. Although I loved the female gender, my priorities were directed at learning my job. I found no one special, so nothing too serious had developed.

Work remained my priority until a routine traffic stop was about to change everything. Routine stops had paid dividends for me. Luckily, I had been able to catch a continuous array of criminal activity during dayshifts. As examples: I had picked up a suspect accused of committing five armed robberies that occurred in Edmonton; several persons with outstanding traffic warrants; a runaway teenage girl; and one missing person who had dementia. Those kinds of results had made me a big fan of routine checks and check stops.

The day in question was filled with a bright sun that was tempered with a fresh summer breeze—the kind of day that made one feel glad to be alive. It was around 10:30 a.m. when I spotted a black pickup truck coming into town. I estimated its speed was over the town speed limit. Although I had no radar reading on the vehicle, I wanted to warn the driver anyway. I completed the routine licence plate check resulting in no wants or warrants being noted. I stopped the truck in a safe area on a side street.

After approaching the truck, I began speaking with the male driver. I noticed throughout the conversation that the female passenger had constantly stared directly at me without blinking. It made me a bit uncomfortable, so I purposely avoided her continuous eye contact.

I gathered the driver's vehicle and operator's licence particulars and then asked the female for her identification. She passed me her operator's licence by reaching directly across the male's chest. She looked deep into my eyes and smiled as her hand touched mine.

While walking back to my vehicle I wondered, *What's with this girl? This seems a bit strange. She is good-looking though!*

I had work to do so I shrugged it off.

I checked both occupants on the police computer system with negative results. No one was wanted in the vehicle. I returned promptly and gave both subjects their particulars. The male driver had been very polite, admitting to the speeding accusation. He was given a verbal warning then sent on his way. He departed as I said, "Have a good day!"

I watched them for a few moments as they drove off. I remained there while writing up my notes on the vehicle stop. This recalled the female's reaction to me. It's always an ego booster when members of the opposite sex pay attention to you. She had definitely paid attention to me. I took time to recall her face and her name. It was Jennifer. She had pleasant features: a dainty nose, and a nice shade of blue in her eyes set off by short stylish dark brown hair. I would have to admit I was attracted to her.

The most important thing I remember was the way that Jennifer looked at me—you know, attracted, as if by the laws of nature—like she had no other choice. In that moment, I wanted to re-stop the truck and act on those emotions. Reality set in as I jolted myself back to thinking w-o-r-k. "If the occasion arises, I may talk to her a little bit more to see if there was actually a connection," I said to myself.

I returned to patrolling the streets. I waved at local friends, ran licence plates from vehicles parked at the bar, and remained on the lookout for anything suspicious. I had just pulled away from another routine vehicle check when the Vermilion detachment office clerk called me on the police radio. Her piercing voice asked, "Constable Mitchell, did you stop a black pickup truck about twenty-five minutes ago for speeding?"

"Yes, I gave them a warning, why?"

"Sergeant Tibber needs you to return to the office right away. He wants to speak to you about the matter."

"10-4," I complied right away, wondering what had happened.

When I opened the detachment door Sergeant Tibber was standing at the front counter with a written complaint in his hands. "You stopped a black pickup for speeding on Nelson Street a short time ago?"

"Yes, I did, what's wrong?"

"The female passenger seems to think you forgot to return her ID."

"Sergeant I'm sure I gave it back to her. I distinctly remember having to reach across the male driver's chest to pass it to her."

"Well, she says you didn't. Go out there and see if you can find them. Straighten it out or I'll have to send the complaint into Edmonton for further investigation."

I was puzzled. *How could this Jennifer say I hadn't given her operator's licence back?* I hunted methodically around town until I spotted the black pickup. I pulled it over again but this time I began to walk up to the passenger's side of the truck.

I glared directly into the side view mirror at Jennifer's eyes. She could see I wasn't happy. Before I was able to utter a word, she spoke up, "I'm very sorry! I just found my licence. It had fallen into another area of my purse so when I couldn't find it, I thought you had forgotten to give it back to me! I'm sorry!"

What could I do then? I couldn't react like I planned. So, in a polite business-like voice I said, "That's okay—but you'll have to go directly to the office to see Sergeant Tibber so he can cancel the complaint against me. Do you understand?"

"Sure, I'll do that right away! I feel bad. I want to make it up to you somehow! Can I buy you a cup of coffee or something? Maybe at Chan's? I am very sorry!"

My first instinct was to refuse the offer, but she seemed to be genuinely sincere. My common sense said, "She just made an honest mistake."

I politely answered "Okay, you go to the office, and I'll see you at Chan's in a few minutes."

The truck pulled away. I felt kind of excited. I had to admit to myself, *I do find this girl attractive, right down to her shoes.*

I continued to feel a sense of anticipation. When I arrived at the restaurant, I picked a table in the corner for some privacy. I ordered coffee and eagerly awaited her arrival.

It took about ten minutes before Jennifer walked into the small one-room restaurant. She smiled again when she spotted me in the corner. She had walked in alone. I got up and stuck out my hand to greet her. I must have looked puzzled, so she explained, "My brother has other things to do in town. He'll be back for me in a little while."

Until that very moment, I hadn't really thought of their relationship when I stopped them. I only knew that they had the same last name. Her address on her licence was in Edmonton and his was Kitscoty. I guess I assumed they were siblings or maybe an estranged or separated couple.

We spoke about the usual things new acquaintances talked about. We spoke of things like where she worked, where I was from, and marital status. You know, all the things all of us need to know to take that "initial attraction" to the next level.

The talk was comfortable and easy. Time elapsed very quickly, a sure sign that we were very compatible. I remember really liking her physically. I even found her voice to be somewhat hypnotic. The whole encounter was invigorating, something I hadn't felt for some time. Without any hesitation, we agreed on an acceptable time for a second meeting. This time it would be a real first date. It would occur when I was off duty the next evening.

The date was even more successful. One thing had led to another. Jennifer and I became a couple seemingly madly in love, or I should say, in lust. It took some time, but I would later find that out, unfortunately. I must admit it was sort of a long-distance relationship though.

She lived and worked in Edmonton, 120 miles away, and I was there, in Vermilion. At first the distance didn't seem to keep us apart. From the very beginning, I commuted to Edmonton to spend time with her regularly. It got so I even commuted between shifts at times. I certainly got my money's worth out of my old Chevy truck.

That fantastic relationship went on for the next three months. I was very happy with Jennifer. She was beautiful, loving, and exciting. In some ways, she changed my life. At the very least, she taught me a lot of new things about women I hadn't known before.

Like all things, when one is young, the day comes when relationships change. We were not immune, so we parted company with very few regrets. I know I have always remembered her in the kindest of ways.

Throughout a police officer's career regardless of the duty or location, there are times when a peace officer receives periodic complaints about his perceived conduct or behaviour. Most times these complaints are unfounded. It usually occurs as the result of a misunderstanding or as a complainant's attempt to get out of a charge or ticket. That is not so say that all complaints against police members are unfounded, because some are real.

As a peace officer, there is a need to develop people skills to deal with the public properly. Even so, things can go awry. It's what makes police work so challenging and so complicated. I can truly say, like most working peace officers, I've received my share of complaints against my perceived conduct throughout the years. Most of them leave unpleasant feelings and a sort of need to re-evaluate your own career choice.

In retrospect, I have recalled Jennifer's complaint against me. I must say it was the best version of a complaint I have ever received.

"Thank-you, Jennifer!"

A Near Miss

SOMETIME IN MAY, Constable Sam Weis, a friend of Tig's, arrived at the detachment from Edmonton. He had worked with Tig at a previous detachment where they became old-time buddies. On that specific dayshift, he decided to work with us that morning. We had spent all day together since 6:00 a.m.

The shift had been especially enjoyable for me that day. I got to observe firsthand another member's point of view and when and what it would be like to have a true partner. I noticed Sam was filled with a refreshing eagerness that translated into bold enthusiasm. I found him to be a very likeable member.

The shift was about to end with only twenty minutes remaining before 4:00 p.m. It had been a quiet day. To wind down, the three of us were standing around at the detachment office trading stories. I should say that Tig and Sam were trading stories. I was listening intently, laughing along with them.

The office phone rang, interrupting the conversation. I took the complaint call from Edmonton Telecoms. A request was made for a rural member to respond to an injury or possible death incident. The location was Paradise Valley. A lady supposedly jumped off a bridge into shallow water bumping her head. The dispatcher indicated she was unconscious and showing very little signs of life.

I handed the phone directly over to Tig. He was the one designated working rural that day. I had never gone to that type of incident, so I asked Sergeant Tibber if I could attend with Tig. He knew my municipal shift was almost over. He thought for a moment, and then gave me the weirdest look.

"No, you must finish your shift on municipal. You're the only one here to cover if a call comes in!"

His response was strange. He knew very well that nothing ever happened around town in the daytime. Since I had been working there, Sergeant Tibber had regularly allowed us to take off ten or fifteen minutes early if we wanted to do something.

Especially on occasions when Tig and I wanted to attend another call together. I couldn't understand his response. It was inconsistent.

"Sergeant, it's less than twelve minutes now! By the time Tig gets his car loaded it'll be 4:00 p.m.—I'd like to go with him to help." I almost begged him. He hesitated again. I could tell he was thinking about something, and for a moment I thought he would see my reasoning and let me attend.

"My decision is firm. You must cover the shift!"

For several moments, I felt like a school kid asking for permission to go to the bathroom. Sam quickly volunteered after hearing Sergeant Tibber's response. I silently relented. I could do nothing but watch Tig and Sam drive off.

For a moment, I quite resented Sam for taking my usual place. I sat there feeling disappointed. I knew I would be missing an exciting experience. The final eight minutes of the shift had elapsed. As I had surmised, nothing had happened by 4:00 p.m. I signed off duty then went to the barracks side of the office to clean up by taking a shower and putting on fresh civilian clothes.

Within a short time, I returned to the office. I was eager to hear anything at all about Tig's call. It was my way of becoming involved.

Thirty-five minutes had elapsed. The office phone rang once again. It was Edmonton Telecoms advising us that Tig and Sam had picked up the lady, who was found alive. While en route to the hospital, their police vehicle was involved in an accident in Lloydminster.

It appeared that Tig had been driving through an intersection a short distance from the hospital when the collision occurred. The report was that both Tig and Sam were seriously injured. All the dispatcher could say was that their car had been wrapped around a traffic light pole. Sam had been crushed in the abdominal pelvic area and Tig had suffered undisclosed internal injuries.

The whole detachment was understandably upset by the bad news. Sergeant Tibber, Corporal Butler, and I jumped into a police vehicle. Before getting to the hospital, the sergeant stopped at the actual scene where the Lloydminster Traffic members were investigating the accident. We all got out and looked at the car. I remember my thoughts of utter disbelief at the sight of the severe damage to the car. It was virtually bent in half around the pole at the centre of the passenger- side's front door. It was just where Sam was sitting. I could only imagine how serious his internal injuries must have been.

After a few more anxious minutes, we entered the hospital where the corporal collected Tig's and Sam's revolvers from a Lloydminster member. They had been taken from them at the hospital for safekeeping.

Due to the serious nature of their injuries, the doctors wouldn't let us see either of them. We were advised that Sam was in severe shock and might not make it through the night. A plan to transport both Tig and Sam by ambulance to Edmonton had been initiated by the hospital. Their survival would depend on how quickly they could be transported. Another doctor confirmed that Tig had back and some internal injuries. Attempts to stabilize him were still ongoing.

During a silent trip back to Vermilion, I suddenly realized what had just happened. On almost every occasion that Tig or I had to attend a call after our shifts we had always gone together. That was regardless of whether either one of us was off duty.

I began to think of how Sergeant Tibber had reacted strangely to my request to attend the call with Tig. I have always had a vivid imagination, but there seemed to be some reason why I wasn't with Tig on that case. I thought very clearly about my personal beliefs of what had just happened. Someone or something had influenced Sergeant Tiber's sudden decision to act against his normal policy.

I went over and over it but came to the same conclusion. I genuinely was concerned about my sudden revelation. Life was fragile; changing one factor like replacing me with Sam could change the whole outcome of his life or my own. The clarity of that moment made me realize, *that should have been me laying in Sam's hospital bed fighting for my life! Is it my imagination or did something intervene like fate or luck—or was it just a coincidence?*

I thought about it for several hours after we arrived back at Vermilion. Between sarge's strange response to my request and Sam's untimely visit that day, I questioned myself, "Am I seeing too much into it or did something save me from that accident?"

I was thankful either way. I decided not to speak about it to anyone. I gradually left the matter alone. I wouldn't think of it again until two other strange incidents occurred to me much later in my career. Once again, I would consider the theory that something intervened to protect me from harm.

After the accident, the whole detachment suffered from shock. I distinctly remember the first night was a restless one for me. In the weeks that followed, things gradually returned to normal.

Remaining busy, the time passed quickly as I continued to work hard. I had visited both Tig and Sam repeatedly. I watched them both gradually recover. I was very pleased when they both eventually were able to return to duty.

As life went on in Vermilion, I had noticed that Tig had become a more cautious driver after that incident. A bit later in my service when I was posted to Airdrie Freeway Patrol, I worked with Sam again. Outwardly, he showed no signs of permanent injury. But my observation was that both Tig and Sam had changed. The shine had worn off their "gung-ho!" along with their "we are invincible" attitudes. That event had changed all of us.

On The Move

TIG AND I WERE ABOUT to sit down in the barracks main recreation room. We were both on a day off. It was shortly after noon when our phone rang. Tig was the closest, so he answered it.

"Mason Mounted Police! Can I help you?"

I watched as he listed to the caller's response. He made several different faces. He looked at me while he spoke to the caller, "Yes Sir! I will do that from now on, Sir. Yes, Sir! He's right here!"

Tig seemed red-faced and embarrassed. I reached out so he could hand me the phone. I grabbed it, covered the mouthpiece with my right hand and whispered, "Who is it?

Tig gave me a strange look and mouthed the words "Staffing Branch."

I was more than a bit curious, so I responded directly. "This is Constable Mitchell. Can I help you?

"This is Inspector Wilson of Staffing in Edmonton. I'm calling to ask if you're interested in accepting a temporary transfer to Jasper National Park detachment. Your role would be in the capacity of performing Red Serge duties."

I answered without an instant of hesitation. "Yes Sir, I would be glad to transfer to Jasper. When would it be effective?"

"Constable Mitchell you're living in the barracks at Vermilion, correct?"

"That's right, Sir!"

"And are you still single at this time?"

"Yes, Sir, that's correct!"

"Well then, you should receive a transfer notice within the week. We need you to start before or on the first of July. Do you see any problem with that?"

I was excited. I'm sure he recognized the enthusiasm in my voice when I answered, "No Sir, there is no problem at all, thank-you very much!"

I hung up the phone and looked directly at Tig as he quietly spoke. "So, you're going to Jasper, are you?" I sensed he seemed a little disappointed by the way he said it. I knew he wished that he had been the one transferred somewhere also.

I couldn't help myself; I was happy. At the same time, I felt a little guilty at the opportunity presented to me. After all, I had only been at Vermilion for six months—just enough time to get comfortable. Vermilion had always offered something to learn, but for some reason, I wholeheartedly embraced the opportunity to transfer to a new posting.

Ever since Tig's police car accident, things hadn't been the same around the detachment. My sense of excitement had been subdued. Staffing's timely proposal of the move to a new duty and location was just what I needed.

I got along with everyone, but I was eager to take what I had learned and apply it to the next place. Due to the law-abiding nature of the good people of Vermilion, serious incidents were rare and occurred infrequently. It being a quiet place, I had always been given ample time to conduct a proper investigation on the files assigned to me. I was unselfishly afforded guidance from both reference materials and the members themselves. I had been able to complete every file by the book.

I didn't realize it then but being posted to Vermilion had given me a solid investigative foundation. A foundation I would use for the rest of my career. Every member of Vermilion had freely given me their time and guidance during my six-month stint as a recruit. It was the most perfect conditions to learn the best investigative techniques.

Negatively, the downside to being posted to a quiet, small, rural detachment was just the fact that it was quiet. Members posted to that type of detachment could tend to become unengaged, complacent, and even impotent, as investigators. Too busy wasn't good and neither was too quiet. I knew if I stayed in Vermilion my experience at some point would become limited.

I aspired to be like the others. I wanted to be looked upon as a seasoned peace officer. In Vermilion, I was known as a recruit. It carried the stigma of being unsure of one's actions, with very little experience. Some would say, "He's still wet behind the ears."

The transfer to Jasper would give me a chance to start at a new place as a regular member—as a member with at least some experience.

Tig and I spoke about Jasper a little longer. I suddenly changed the topic. There was something else I was curious about. "Tig, why the funny looks after you answered the phone?"

"What do you mean?"

"You know what I mean."

"Tim! It was nothing."

"Come on, can you tell me?"

"Well, your buddy, Inspector Wilson, didn't quite like the way I answered the phone."

"What do you mean?" I asked him the question although I was quite sure what he was about to say. After a tense moment or two more he blurted out the answer.

"I didn't state my rank before my name or say Royal Canadian Mounted Police when I answered."

Deep down I knew that was it. I had witnessed Sergeant Tibber giving Tig the same chastising in the office on previous occasions. I remained silent. I was aware Tig had been trying to get a transfer for a long time. Here I was just finished my training. Now I suddenly had a great transfer to Jasper National Park. I didn't want to rain on his parade, so I remained unresponsive to his last statements.

Tig couldn't take the silence, so he defended his actions by attacking the officer rank for their pettiness regarding proper practices.

"Those officer types have nothing more to do than to pick on such foolish things." Everyone knows who the Mounted Police are!"

I shook my head in agreement only to placate Tig. Deep down I knew that the RCMP was a semi-military organization. I personally could see nothing wrong with adhering to the RCMP's proper practices. Nevertheless, I had no intention of jeopardizing my friendship with Tig over such a matter.

I managed to change the subject by suggesting that we go to Chan's Restaurant to celebrate; the lunch being on me. He agreed, so off we went for lunch.

The news of my impending transfer quickly circulated through the detachment office staff. The news hadn't taken long before it spread like a virus throughout the whole town and outlying areas.

Within a couple of days, I was routinely stopped by numerous Vermilion residents wishing to make some comment to me about my transfer to Jasper. There were those I hadn't even met before who graciously approached me with unexpected favourable comments. Their positive statements and reactions to the transfer came as a complete surprise. They repeated compliments that they had about me as being a valuable and trustworthy constable, and regretted I had to leave. It was somewhat overwhelming for me. By the end of my time in Vermilion I was sure I would have to order an extra hat size if it kept up. I even found handwritten notes left on my truck from three young girls I hadn't met, asking me to marry them before I left.

I didn't quite understand it at the time, but on my trip to Jasper, I finally figured it out. In every small rural town, there are always several girls who will marry almost anyone as a way to get out of town. I'm not suggesting that some of the Mounties that had married girls from a small town weren't really in love. Those Mounties had dated and courted their respective wives over a period. I hadn't even met those three girls. So, I concluded my hypothesis was most likely correct.

I never expected any acknowledgement of my work. I wasn't in the Force to attain glory for an expected behaviour. The final few days were filled with humbling experiences. There was nothing more gratifying than being trusted as a peace officer. I remained grounded by remembering privately that all of us at the detachment were thought of the same way. We were all just doing our jobs.

I received my transfer notice, as promised, within the next week's period. The orders read: Constable Mitchell is to report to Jasper detachment by June 28, 1976, for duty. After the standard ritual of a "transfer party," I said my good-byes.

The next morning, I packed up my Chevy truck before anyone had gotten up. With one more look back at Vermilion, I turned onto the Trans-Canada Highway. I stepped on the gas pedal to speed up. A bittersweet feeling came over me as I travelled down the road towards Jasper.

I was alone and heading for higher ground. The long trip gave me time to ponder the Vermilion experience. Good feelings of well-being remained throughout the whole drive. I reflected on the compliments from the citizens of Vermilion. I was determined not to take it too seriously. I only allowed myself a short time to smile about it all and just feel good. I knew my Dad and Mom would be proud of me if they had known.

I urged my thoughts to the next challenge: Jasper detachment and "Red Serge Duties."

Within five hours I found myself entering the main gates of Jasper National Park. I had to indicate that I was about to take up residence in Jasper as a peace officer. On that note, the National Parks Officer asked to see my handgun to ensure that it had been safely transported, unloaded with a seal attached through the barrel. He waved me through welcoming me to my new posting.

The sky was clear, and the sun was pleasantly hot. The smell of summer permeated the air. I saw movement and life everywhere. Whenever I had driven into the mountains of Alberta, it made me feel great. I loved the mountains.

It brought back a forgotten memory of the first time I visited Jasper. It had been nine years earlier. The year was 1967.

My younger brother, Steve, and I had convinced our parents that we would be able to safely take the train across Canada and back. It would be our "Centennial Project." We were proud New Brunswickers but even more proud as Canadian. Canada's one hundredth birthday was something to celebrate.

We were both in those middle teenage years—fifteen and sixteen. It was a delicate time. We were not yet men and not just boys anymore. Even so, Steve and I were ready to spread our wings a little. After making a solemn promise to phone home each day, our father agreed to let us go on the trip. We contrived a scheme to save money on the calls home. One of us would call person to person and ask for Tim Mitchell. My father would routinely answer the phone each night giving the same answer— "Tim Mitchell isn't here right now."

The person-to-person routine allowed our family to hear our voices when we asked for Tim Mitchell and our family knew we were safe at no cost to them or us.

The trip had turned out to be fantastic. We both enjoyed the uniqueness of each location. Every place presented something special. At the trip's conclusion, reality set in. This had been "a trip of a lifetime."

It had expanded my view of Canada. I was left in a state of awe and wonder at the vastness and diversity we encountered. My chest was filled with pride.

"I was actually part of such a great country!"

From that time on, Canada was my first home and New Brunswick became my second. I no longer regarded myself as being from New Brunswick. I belonged to something much bigger. I was a Canadian, proud to have been born in such a wonderful country.

Jasper was one of those special places. A two-day visit wasn't enough. I loved everything about the place. Somehow it held a magical fixation for me. Immediately after I stepped down from the train an overwhelming feeling of being at the right place filled my mind. It was love at first sight. When our short visit came to an end, I vowed to return to it someday.

I abruptly returned to reality when I saw an elk on the roadway standing directly in my path. I slammed on my brakes, skidding about five car lengths before stopping directly in front of that majestic monster. The elk was unafraid. It stood its ground. I could do nothing but stare at the piercing eyes and giant rack of horn of the foreboding creature that stood before me.

What was I to do? What was the proper thing to do?

I fumbled through my brain trying to find a plausible answer. The elk was waiting, and I waited, transfixed. Suddenly we were both startled by the blasting sound of a semi-tractor trailer unit's horn. It startled both of us simultaneously. I cringed as it barrelled past at a high speed on the left side of my truck. The elk moved abruptly, turning its head away from me, and I inadvertently stepped on the gas driving directly forward towards it. Miraculously, we missed each other in our attempts to escape the predicament. In that moment, I was sure I was going to hit the elk. To my surprise, it vanished as if into thin air. I found myself driving back on the road, shaken but unharmed.

So here it was the end of June 1976. I arrived at the detachment with little or no problem by following the well-placed RCMP signs throughout the town. I walked into the front office after parking my truck at the rear. I was impressed at the overall design and location of the detachment. It looked just like a hunting lodge. It stood majestically in a meadow-like setting that backed onto a mountain instead of a tiny city lot. I found the building as beautiful inside as it appeared outside. I was excited at my new posting.

Entering the town site had produced the feelings I had expected. My longtime wish to live and work in Jasper had been completed. All was well with me on that day. I remained without any doubts, I still loved Jasper. It was a jewel I would never forget. It was by far the most enjoyable posting of my career.

Throughout my working life, I had often recalled its many pleasant memories. At times, a specific memory that was thought to be forgotten, kindly popped up to be fondly relived.

I was greeted politely by the civilian clerk. I identified myself and he acknowledged I had been expected. Within a few seconds, I found myself standing in front of Staff Sergeant Benson Johannes.

He was not at all like Sergeant Tibber. He wore the uniform well, appearing very fit. He had an organized office and projected the air of a boss comfortable with his role in the Force.

"Here are my transfer papers Staff. I'm Tim Mitchell from Vermilion."

"You can sit down if you'd like, Tim." He pointed to the chair to my right.

I said, "Thanks!" as I sat down. While he looked at my papers, I was struck by his calm laid-back attitude. I liked that he used my first name instead of my rank as constable.

"I'm Benson Johannes, I'm in charge of Jasper detachment, and on behalf of the members and staff, I want to welcome you."

"Thanks, Staff!"

"Tim, there's no need to call me Staff when we're here out of the public's eye. Ben will suffice. Now tell me a bit about yourself—I know you're from New Brunswick and that you did very well during your Recruit Field Training period. Your trainer, Mel, sent me the details yesterday."

I replied by telling him some pertinent facts about myself. I felt reasonably sure they were things he already knew. He came across as a very polite and gracious man. My sense about him told me he was more like my trainer, Mel, that I could have ever hoped. With the initial formalities out of the way, it was down to business.

"Tim, I want to tell you what your role will be here."

"Okay."

"First of all, you do know that this is a temporary transfer?"

"Yes. How long will it be—just the summer?"

"You are here specifically for Red Serge Duty. This will include all summer until sometime into the early fall—just for the tourist season."

"So that should be for about five months?"

Staff Johannes ignored the question and stayed on point with his speech.

"You will most likely get transferred again shortly afterward. Unfortunately, all the positions at this detachment are filled at the moment. The federal government has paid for two of you to be here to enhance Jasper's tourist industry."

I nodded to indicate I understood.

"It will be your duty to meet as many tourists as you can each day. Remember, you will be representing the Royal Canadian Mounted Police at its best—so it's very important that your behaviour and presence in public remain beyond reproach. Is that clear Tim?"

"Yes, Staff."

"I still want to complete the whole picture for you. I have had first-hand experience with Red Serge duty. It was on Parliament Hill a few years ago, but nothing has changed. It's not an easy job! You will meet between 400 to 500 tourists a day. They will include persons from all walks of life, from all cultures, and from all over the world. Everyone will want pictures of you, to stand beside you, and sometimes even hug and kiss you. Your shifts will be full and exhausting. Then there are those tourists that will want more!"

I nodded again.

"Tim, it's important to make the best decision for the Force and for you when faced with tourists like that. Do you understand what I mean?"

"I think so Staff?"

"I'm sure you'll figure it out! But let's look on the positive sides of the duty. I really expect you to do a great job for us. Judging from what Mel has written everything should work out just fine."

"Thank-you again Staff."

"But, if you have any problems please don't hesitate to come in and talk to me about them.

"And—before I forget it. On the odd day, when it rains, don't bother getting your Stetson wet; consider taking the rest of that day off or adjust your shift to fit the weather. When you run into a group of persons or even one person that you connect with, it'll be all right to let them buy you lunch, if they wish. In some situations, like when a group of tourists want you to accompany them on the Sky Tram or go with them on the Maligne Lake tour, it will be your decision. You will be provided with a free pass on all the facilities here in Jasper.

I want you to give us one hundred percent, but I also want you to enjoy your duty. These types of opportunities usually come once in a member's career. I trust you will take this role seriously Tim. Remember. Meet and communicate the positives of the Force to as many tourists as possible during your shifts. Have fun with it all! Can I count on you to do that?"

"Yes sir, I'll do my best!"

"Oh! I forgot to tell you, Kye Burnston, will be sharing this duty with you. He's not in right now. I'll try to introduce you a little later. He's from Saint John, New Brunswick and he even has about your service. I trust that both of you will have a lot in common to talk about?"

With that he summoned Bob Curtain, a civilian employee, to complete the office tour. During our walk-about, I met several other members, the guard, and of course, the dayshift clerk. Bob even provided me with my proposed schedule, which indicated I'd be working on the first of July. I really loved everyone's friendly attitude, but especially the fantastic layout of the place.

It looked and felt just like being in a hunting lodge. It even had the RCMP trademark of the day, a gigantic bison head hung on one of the main office walls. The whole décor presented the image of a real expensive late 1960s' hunting lodge or private retreat.

I sure could get used to living here! I thought to myself. *It's like a dream come true.*

I was soon to find it was even better than that. Much to my satisfaction, the single men's quarters turned out to be individual lockable rooms. Upon entering my assigned room, I was astonished. It was made up like a hotel room, with an individual private bathroom. It was far more comfortable than the barracks set-up at most detachments. At most places, members were forced to share the same bedrooms and a single bathroom.

Later that afternoon, I started to come down from the long trip. It had been a full first day at Jasper. I found myself lying on my freshly laundered bed sheets in my very quiet private room. I pondered how hard it would be to go back to sharing the one-room barracks thing. The office was a gem all right!

It really wasn't until several years had passed before I really understood how good I had it when posted at Jasper. Close to the end of my career, I had occasion to remember all the great bosses I had worked for throughout my service. I recalled there were many, but Staff Sergeant Ben Johannes stood out as being the best supervisor I ever had. He was the kind of man to look up to and to aspire to become. I loved my time in Jasper for many reasons. Ben was undoubtedly the number one reason on my list.

The next morning, I awoke at about 6:00 a.m. I got dressed in fresh civilian clothes. I was eager to have breakfast. I met with the office clerk, who reminded me that I had two days to settle in before attending the July 1st Canada Day Ceremony at the Jasper Park Lodge in Red Serge. I was told Kye and I would be attending with a third senior constable, Kurt Flemming. He was another member of the Jasper detachment. Since Kye and I were somewhat unfamiliar with the process, Flemming would act as a guide. He was another Jasper member who had experience with those types of ceremonial events.

After getting all of that straight, I wandered to the coffee room of the detachment to see if I could meet some other members. I was thinking I could convince someone else to join me for breakfast. I walked in on four of them sitting at the table having coffee. I introduced myself, with each of them returning a gesture. As had happened in Vermilion, they all took their turn subtly asking me for background information. I complied, and to my surprise found it easier than the Vermilion experience. I guessed that with each transfer it would get easier.

To my surprise, Constable Kye Burnston arrived in the room a short time later looking like he had had a rough night of it. The other members had met Kye the night before and took him out on the town. He appeared to still be a little hazy.

The Staff Sergeant was right, Kye had about my service. We were in training at Depot Division at the same time. I hadn't known him as he was in a different troop of recruits. Nevertheless, we hit if off quite nicely. Being New Brunswickers, we had a lot in common, the same feeling for home; we both liked Dulse Seaweed and we had similar upbringings with many other siblings. Right away I felt we could work together and have loads of fun doing it.

During my time in Jasper, I found all the staff and members at the attachment to be friendly without exception.

In the days that followed, I would come to realize public relations of that type was definitely a two-sided coin. Although it was enjoyable, it was exhausting. Especially when we were continuously being compelled to say just the right thing in just the right way.

I remember initially thinking, *I'll never get used to this!* To my error, after the first week passed, I got the hang of it. I amazed myself. In a very short time, I became very comfortable—almost too comfortable. I was transformed into an actor with such confidence that any previous inhibitions of performing before strangers had long since vanished. As "Mountie on Display" though, some days could be stressful. I knew Staff Johannes had been clear about what to expect. I had listened to every word of his welcoming speech. Even so, I had no real idea the extent of the loss of privacy in the form of adulation one received when dressed in the red uniform of the Royal Canadian Mounted Police. I was honoured to be representing one of the most world's recognized icons of Canada. It seemed that people from all nations, be they from Ceylon to America, honoured the RCMP.

CHAPTER 16

An Added Bonus

ABOUT A MONTH AND A half into Red Serge Duty, I was able to anticipate what most tourists wanted in advance. I could tell some were amazed when I suggested what they wanted before they could ask. It was like a magic trick for the tourists. Both parties involved had a lot of fun with it. So, the game went on.

I also began to play a personal game. The game was guessing where each tourist came from originally. I based my guess solely upon hearing their accents from the first few initial words of contact. I played the game with everyone I met during my shift.

The first two weeks I was only approximately twenty percent correct with my guesses. When the hundreds of guesses became thousands of guesses I became consistently correct until I recognized accents of persons from every province in Canada and about seventy-five percent of the states in the US. In addition, I could get about eighty percent of the Western European accents correct, as well as the accents of persons from Ceylon, India, Japan, Korea, China, Australia, New Zealand, South

Africa, Russia, Scandinavia, South America, Mexico, And the Eastern bloc countries of Romania, Hungary, and Czechoslovakia.

I especially became adept at detecting the unique American accents of people from Texas, New York, the Carolinas, the Mid-West, Florida, Georgia, and Louisiana etc.

Although that ability sounds like a fairy tale, it was very true. It came about solely by trial and error. I practiced the game with a minimum of two hundred people daily. I worked twenty-two days a month, eight hours a day for five months. The simple math can give you a phenomenal number of guesses. That, in turn, developed an ear for accents. It was an unexpected gift from the Jasper experience. I took every opportunity use it throughout the rest of my career. I can recall numerous occasions where I used it to place persons from other cultures at ease, especially when interviewing them for offences or crimes. Knowing where a subject came from allowed me to solve certain issues concerning cultural differences. I'm referring to the kinds of differences that could explain why distinct types of evidence were found at some murder scenes. Sometimes distinct evidence points to a suspect from a certain culture or nationality.

What culture would a viable suspect come from if he/she placed coins on the eyes of a victim, or left cigarettes or some form of tobacco on or near an otherwise completely naked victim? Or, especially, from what nationality or culture could a viable suspect be if the murderer left the victim with a large stone placed within her chest?

None of these examples have fixed answers. I have listed them to illustrate how unique evidence left at a crime scene may aid the investigator in seeking a potential suspect. It all starts with the accent recognition to determine from where the parties involved originated.

We all know most murderers aren't very smart, as a large majority still get apprehended by leaving very basic evidence behind, like fingerprints, footprints, and their DNA. I also admit that the answers to the three examples are very rudimentary. Even so, I am not about to reveal the answers to the examples. This type of knowledge should be kept for police investigators and forensic specialists so evidence of this nature can continue to be used to solve crimes or potentially produce viable suspects.

The recognition of accents also aided me immensely when conversing with victims. Letting them know right away that I recognized their accent and where they were from always set them at ease. It created a common connection point. The victim always seemed to get the feeling I understood their culture. Letting them know I understood where they were from helped me project the compassion and the best intentions when trying to deliver them assistance.

In the five months, the number of people I conversed with was 16,500 persons. From that extensive experience, I learned to affiliate the unique way people pronounce our English words with a country or specific place. Again, I know it sounds impossible, but by countless hours of trial-and-error guessing, I developed an ear for accents. It was like Red Serge duty placed me on an in-depth course of voice recognition. It wasn't really braining surgery. I always chalked it up to trial and error. This unexpected skill development aided me in obtaining co-operation in countless incidents throughout the rest of my career.

My developed skill of accent recognition had the effect of being a catalyst for me for an in-depth interest in the cultures of the world. It was a subject in which I was keenly interested.

After leaving Jasper, I began a personal study of different cultures and their many customs and beliefs., and my knowledge of ethnic groups increased as I moved from one posting to another throughout Canada. I don't use it for work now but still enjoy its use on occasion.

Or especially, from what nationality or culture could a viable suspect be if the murderer left the victim with a large stone placed within her chest?

Embracing the Role

Serge Duty was hard work like the Staff Sergeant had indicated. It was also exhausting. Even when I had considered those two points, I had to say it was one of the most enjoyable postings of my career. To feel the respect and the trust from the people of the world was astounding. I believed it was the fact that I was a real Mountie present in the flesh, standing before them. They could talk with me and even touch me to see that I was real. The Mounties had a reputation of being beyond reproach. Our uniform and members were treated as icons for Canada in the 1960s and 1970s. At the end of some days, I experienced brief moments of thinking I should just run away. Of course, my curiosity helped me stand fast. I wanted to see what was about to occur. The interpreter must have seen the look in my eyes. He quickly yelled something, and the group kept coming, but laughed, then changed their pace to a slow walk. Individuals from the crowd took turns asking me in broken English to have a picture taken with me. I readily agreed to comply with their requests.

Once again, I was surprised. Instead of standing alone with each person or couple, one man in the party volunteered to take over one hundred cameras around his neck to complete the request. When about half of the group deposited their cameras, the elderly gentleman began to wobble under the weight. I heard him say something to the group. They all stopped. That allowed him to take off the cameras as he carefully placed each camera, as if it was his own, on the ground in front of him. The group seemed very willing to comply. Each person filed by the man in an unexpected orderly fashion, each taking their turn placing a camera on the ground in front of him. I remember that the vision of the crowd's-controlled movements made me think I was watching some type of sacred ritual in some foreign land. Once the cameras were laid out, the final few stragglers joined all of those that surrounded me. I began to feel them squeezing in around me so tightly that I thought my hat would surely pop off at any moment. The 149 individuals all wanted to make sure they were included in the picture. I stood patiently at attention while members of the group pushed and pulled each other to get as close to me as possible. At the time, I guessed it was so they could claim their picture was taken with the Mountie and not the other heads that bobbed in the photograph. I was astonished at the man's perseverance. He clicked and clicked until all the cameras had taken at least one photograph of the group. He went on for at least twenty minutes.

Most times the end of the day, I stood in the shower with a sense of awe about the respect people had for the RCMP. Red Serge duty gave me an immeasurable experience of a lifetime. In that short summer, my life went from zero to sixty in the wink of an eye. I learned so much about people, trust, politics, ethnic difference, personal and public relationships, and most of all about the "Power of the Red Serge" when interacting with the female sex. At times the women's reactions, regardless of their ages, became a bit overwhelming. Their reactions were so varied it was impossible at first to know just what to expect. Some would gently caress my arm, shoulder, or hand while posing with me for a photograph. Some would propose on the spot without realizing that their spouses were standing within earshot taking the photograph. At times conversations were more direct than they should have been. I remember my first day on Red Serge Duty. I was dropped off at the Jasper Park Lodge where an oilman convention was in session. As I walked about the Lodge, I greeted passersby with a smile and a quiet hello.

I was stopped on several occasions to answer questions and pose with individuals for photographs when requested. It was a dreamlike feeling for me the first few times. I had to ask myself, "Why would anybody want to ask me any questions or take a picture of me?"

It seemed astounding to me at the time. I soon came to realize that the power of the image of the world-recognized Mountie was beyond any one individual's control. I learned to just go along with it and to hang on tightly to the experiences that would influence me the rest of my career.

I can't speak for anyone else who has worked Red Serge duty in the Force. I only know that it was a truly uplifting experience in the mid 1970s. I was single, and Jasper was a beautiful vibrant place with great summer weather. There were loads of fantastic women from all over the world who happened to find a Mountie dressed in the red coat attractive and interesting.

During the first several encounters, the succession of inquisitors was very polite and gracious in their exchanges with me. Just after leaving a nice couple from Britain, I began to proceed from the main great room down a hallway leading to the conference room area of the Jasper Park Lodge. The doors to the room suddenly burst open. Streams of people in couples poured into the hallway. I watched the stampede in both amazement and with some trepidation. I was some distance down the narrow hallway so I couldn't do anything but step to one side and let the herd of conventioneers' pass. The group moved towards me as if escaping a burning building. I stepped to the extreme edge of the hallway, backing myself up against the wall to allow the throng to pass. I was continuously being acknowledged with a momentary look and a nod. The continuous droning sound of many conversations filled the hallway as they passed.

All was going fine when I heard the loud voice of a woman in her late fifties. It was plain to me she had overindulged. The slurring tones in her words were distinctly evident. I watched her clinging to a large bald man smoking a cigar. He afforded her the tight grip of stability as they walked. She hadn't noticed me at first, but as the room emptied, her conversation stopped abruptly as our eyes met. I was about ten feet from her location with nothing between us to obstruct our individual views. She seemed to instantly sober. Her voice became clear of slurring. Her bald crutch was no longer required. She was miraculously able to stand and walk on her own. Her symptoms of impairment had simply vanished into thin air at my sight.

I was intrigued. Could the sight of a Mountie in Red Serge really make people sober up instantly? Of course, I was joking, but nevertheless this was a new experience for me, and I was about to be further astounded. She turned into a woman on a mission. In a few short seconds, she was standing about two feet in front of me. Her eyes were filled with something special and unique. It was "The Look." I would later come to recognize it as that special initial attraction one sometimes gets. It's somehow brought on by our basest natural animal urges that we all have within us. She stood speechless for a few seconds then in a very loud voice blurted out, "How fast can you get your boots off?" I was caught completely off guard; I didn't quite know how to react to this bold unexpected question. I knew exactly what she meant. I was sure I had turned four shades of red while stammering to tell her as politely as possible that we didn't do that sort of thing. Her immediate response was, "We'll see about that!" I could say nothing to that response, so I bid them good day and departed uncomfortably.

I had time to reflect on what had just happened about an hour later. I was embarrassed but intrigued. After all, the encounter did make me feel good about myself. I started looking forward to the possibilities of other encounters like that during the rest of the summer. To stay focussed on this one incident, I should confess that the lady did get her way before the convention was over. She arranged the situation and the place, which was out of my control. We spent several beautiful hours together. I thought about the whole incident later. I came to the realization that she wasn't really enamoured by me. I was sure it was only because I was a Mountie in a red uniform. I was young and single then. She claimed to be single too. Was it a plausible claim? I don't really know. I only know that she was attractive and interested. She made me feel good and the time we spent together made me appreciate the opposite sex even more. As far as I could tell we both won with having met.

CHAPTER 17

Not Really a Ten

THE FEMALE CONTACT I JUST described sounds grand. During my tenure at Jasper, many encounters went as described. I remember one special event that had a totally unexpected ending. I was working another sunny shift on a day when temperatures had risen from seventy-five to eighty degrees by the time noon struck the clock. I had been walking and talking to individuals while making my way down one of the streets to find some actual cover from the exhausting heat. Anyone who has worn their Red Serge in that kind of temperature can understand the uncomfortable feeling. The ceremonial Red Serge uniform included the tight-fitting woolen serge and dark blue woolen riding breaches, along with knee-high, tight-fitting leather boots. To describe them as uncomfortable in those temperatures was an understatement. I was trying my best to wade through the crowd to make shade before sundown. I was periodically stopped to comply with photo requests.

The tourist traffic had swelled that day to the maximum. I don't think the streets could have held another person. Every seat in every restaurant was filled. The businesses shared the same fate. There were literally hundreds of persons on the streets. I paused a moment and looked around. I saw people of every shape, size, and colour. I stopped to listen at the sounds in the air. I heard a conglomerate of languages being spoken aloud. I noticed that the aggregate of chatter had blended into a strange sort of music. The voices from so many countries created a sort of multilingual song that I enjoyed but couldn't understand. It was mid-July. I had never seen so many tourists in such a small space. I watched as they all clambered for anything they could take back with them as a souvenir. Even I was grabbed at times—they pushed, tapped, and poked. One or two individuals even tried to pull some of my buttons off my red serge as a souvenir. I was usually friendly, but not when it came to that behaviour. Every effort was made by the visitors to divert my attention to themselves as individuals.

I began to feel a bit like the subject of a feeding frenzy. The crowd seemed to be getting out of control. At times, I felt I was the only police-man trying to control a riot. I wanted to call it quits but it was still early in the day. I convinced myself to maintain my position as a tourist attrac-tion. After all, they just wanted to get their photograph standing with a Canadian Mountie.

I had just finished pushing my way to the corner of the street where Smitty's Restaurant was located. That vantage point provided me with a real breathtaking view of the hordes of tourists that had invaded Jasper that day. While I was scanning people jamming up against each other, I spotted something unusual through the crowded street beyond, about half a block away. I saw a girl I believed to be between eighteen and twenty-two. She caught my eye. There was something about her that stood out from the crowd.

She was like a diamond shining in the sand. As I watched her approach, our eyes made contact. The vision of that beauty was almost magical. She smiled at me. Our eyes were transfixed, at least on my part. I became almost oblivious to the others around me. I heard voices asking ques-tions, but I ignored them. I believed her to be one of the most beautiful women I'd ever seen in my entire life.

Our eyes remained transfixed on each other. I was sure she was purposefully walking directly towards my position. The closer she came, the better she looked. I was almost mesmerized by the beauty of the girl's eyes and face. I felt embarrassed that I was so taken by her. When she was about six to eight feet in front of me, pushing through the crowd, I looked around me. Everyone was staring at her like I had been. Most of them with mouths open in amazement.

It was then that I noticed a dishevelled male with a beard pulling at her one arm. He seemed to be trying to stop her from meeting me. My common sense kicked in. I recognized something was wrong with that assumed connection between two people.

I convinced myself to be cautious. I remembered how strange the situation had become. The closer she got the more desperate he became. I watched as she walked right up to me. She stopped just short of our noses touching. We stared into each other's eyes as if we were long lost lovers. She was so hypnotic. I have never remembered what she or I talked about in those short minutes. I only know we communicated at the most basic and most understood level. We both knew we should be together. She was downright beautiful in every way.

As we stood face to face, I began to sober from her uncanny beauty. A red flag went up, regardless of how enamoured I had been. It was waving right in front of me. I could see her eyes were glazed over. I knew she was under the influence of something. As she spoke with a soft convincing voice and those blue eyes, part of me said, "It didn't matter!" For a moment or two, I thought I was in love, or maybe it was that other four-letter "l" word.

Within another blink, the encounter ended as her buddy finally convinced her it was time to leave. He kept yanking on her blouse sleeve while repeatedly saying, "We've got to go!"

Finally, it was over. She said good-bye, leaving me with the feeling that we would get together later. As she walked away, I noticed one of our senior female members sitting in a marked police vehicle, watching the action with a smile. By the time I looked back, "Beauty" had walked out of sight with the bad guy. I still remember thinking, *Wow!* When I looked around me, it seemed that hundreds of people had witnessed our magical encounter because some of them cheered when I started moving down the street.

Before I realized it, the shift was over. After returning to the office, I showered, and made ready to go out on the town. Two of the female tourists, a Kate, and a Maggie from Australia, had made arrangements with me to have dinner and drinks that evening. Red Serge duty arbitrarily provided me with choices of female companionship every day. Many female tourists were enamoured by the thought of going out with a Mountie, so those situations happened on a regular basis. To be clear, it was rarely my idea. The women I met during my duty decided when and where the dinner and drink dates would take place. There were times I thought I was breaking the rules the staff sergeant had laid out for me. I finally understood those persons who suffer from being agoraphobic. I had only felt a momentary twinge of it that one time, but it was enough for me.

Then, I remembered him saying, "When someone that you happen to connect with comes along feel free to spend time with her. If a tourist or group of tourists want to buy you lunch let them! Tim, just don't do anything that will bring the Force into ill-repute!"

Recalling his words justified my actions completely, at least back then. While I was getting ready, I felt determined that I should try to seek out the beauty I met that afternoon. I was really curious to find out what happened to her after our encounter.

I was about to leave when the senior female member I spoke about earlier approached me. She asked, "Are you going to look for that beautiful girl you were nose to nose with earlier?"

I was astonished and flattered at the same time. It stuck me odd that she took an interest in who I met on the street.

I replied, "Yes! Maybe!"

She abruptly stated, "Follow me!

We walked from the barracks area through the office. When we started to enter the cells, I blurted out.

"You've got to be kidding?"

She explained that she and Constable Arthur had received a tip just after the girl left my location.

I had to ask. "What was the tip?"

"Yes, when we followed it up, your 'beautiful girl' had been selling marijuana in baggies at twenty dollars a pop. They were standing in full view, as bold as can be, offering the baggies for sale to the tourists. I guess they thought you were the only Mountie in town. Constable Arthur busted them himself. I took care of the last tourist that purchased some weed. I caught him just as he started to walk away."

"So where was this?"

"The take-down occurred about four blocks from where you were last talking to her near Smitty's Restaurant. Both were in possession of cocaine, weed oil, and crystal methamphetamines! It was in the guy's backpack."

The conversation stopped abruptly. The constable began to open the small viewing window in the solid door leading into the female cell area. She peered in ahead of me to make sure the suspect was decent.

"Take a look through the window and see your beautiful girl now that she's coming down from the coke. It's only been four hours now!"

I quickly peered through the glass for another chance to see the girl who had impressed me. I couldn't believe my eyes. It was the same girl alright, but she was dirty, deflated, ordinary, and almost ugly.

Her face had changed. It was no longer glowing. She had deep lines in her face and dark circles under her eyes. I stepped back. My immediate response was, "How could she have changed so much in a few hours?"

"Cocaine does that! When you're on it, you're great, but off it you become you in your lowest form."

I never let the other member know how stupid I felt about almost screwing up my career. I'm sure she noticed.

I secretly thanked my lucky stars that fate intervened. It might sound like utter nonsense, but their timely arrest possibly saved me from a career-alternating incident or even worse, personal danger. It made me mindful of the many things I had yet to learn. My limited list of police experience in Vermilion was far from adequate. It would take many more experiences to remove the thick wrapping of naivete that had protected me as a civilian.

I was amazed at the cultural differences between North Americans and Japanese groups. One morning, I had been assigned to meet a group of Japanese tourists arriving by train, as part of the Jasper Greeting Committee. When the train master began to allow passengers to disembark, the three of us watched in amazement. An endless stream of passengers gathered beside the train station on the platform filling it to overflowing along its complete length. Passengers kept on disembarking continuously until their amount seemed uncountable. In the end, a Japanese interpreter with a group advised us in English there were 150 individuals visiting Jasper.

I listened as he turned to the crowd and spoke in their native tongue. Directly after he stopped speaking, all the passengers simultaneously bowed towards us in honour. We instinctively bowed back.

Like a well-choreographed drill team maneuver, the complete group began to move directly towards me as one mass. Usually, couples insisted on having their own picture taken with me without interference or inclusion of others, but this time was different.

I had done my best to impress the tourists by remaining pleasant, helpful, and professional under an array of circumstances and potential misunderstandings. While on duty, I made it my sole purpose to live up to the legend that tourists from around the world had brought with them. That legend indicated the Royal Canadian Mounted Police was the best police force in the world. Its members were known to always get their man, to always "Maintain the Right," and to be fair and just to victim and culprit alike. Members of the Force could be trusted to do the right thing every time. Those ideas had been demonstrated to me every day by the words and actions of the thousands of tourists I met while posted in Jasper. It certainly made me proud to be an RCMP member. In fact, the exposure in that role accomplished more than that for me as a peace officer. As corny as it sounds, the experience made me promise to myself that I would continue to be the kind of peace officer that embraced those attributes in the legend.

CHAPTER 18

Periwinkles

ONE EVENING, KYE BURNSTON, THE other member working Red Serge Duty, and I had no plans to go out for the night. I guess we were both just too exhausted to attend another party. We agreed to meet in the main office after freshening up with a hot shower and a new set of clothes.

I think I might have mentioned earlier, Kye and I were both from New Brunswick. He had just received a grocery bag full of an edible type of dried seaweed called "dulse" from his parents. Both of us had grown up eating the stuff as a treat. Even so, a full grocery bag was a lot of dulse seaweed to eat alone, so Kye was more than happy to share some with me.

The colours of the very salty seaweed range from black to purple. Easterners harvest dulse by scraping the floating seaweed directly into boats from the sea just off the coast of Grand Manan Island. Once harvested, it's hung on old pieces of netting suspended from stakes driven into a beach to allow a natural drying process. The dulse is bagged unwashed and sold directly as is. Because of this processing procedure it is always speckled with bits of sand and foreign material, with the odd periwinkle attached. The mixture looks inedible to most other Canadians. Although I've seen it written somewhere that periwinkles are edible, the condition of the periwinkles in dulse are nothing more than small sandy shells containing dried dead snails. Most of us would never eat them, so it's the custom to scrape these creatures from the seaweed leaves before eating the dulse.

On that evening, we were sitting in the quiet office of the Jasper detachment sharing the dulse while talking about home and friends. Everyone from the office had gone for the day, leaving a skeleton crew to work nightshift. Jan, the one-night stenographer, and two scheduled nightshift members were the only ones on duty. The members were out on patrol.

We sat eating and talking within a few feet of Jan's desk. She watched us curiously from her workstation. After a short time, she politely interrupted our conversation, "What is that stuff you guys are eating? It looks so black—what is it?"

To this day, I don't know why we did it. Maybe it was because we knew her as extremely gullible. Then maybe it was a bit of mischief that suddenly overruled our common sense. I'm still not too sure who had come up with the idea, but within the seconds it had taken to answer her question, a planned response just automatically fell into place.

The two of us began explaining what dulse was, how it tasted, and how it was harvested. We continued with the description, feeding off each other's explanation. We continually interrupted each other in a timely fashion, painting the following picture.

I could tell she was about to ask why I was collecting the periwinkle shells and placing them aside on a nearby table. Like a bolt of lightning that came out of nowhere I said, "The best part of eating dulse was the periwinkles!" Kye confirmed my statement, indicating that those little snail shells were the most coveted part of eating dulse. Without any doubt, we convinced her periwinkles were some sort of delicacy. She asked us, and then began to almost beg us, to share a few of the periwinkles with her.

We were not expecting that reaction. We really expected an "Awk!" "Ugh!" or a "Yuk!" but she genuinely wanted some. For a moment, we went silent. I really don't know why we hadn't stopped the event right there, but on it went. I reached over and picked up a handful of periwinkles. I gently placed about seven of them in her right hand.

I really expected her to realize that these were seashells. They were hard shells with a dried-up dead snail inside. In the blink of an eye, before either of us could say anything more, she popped the periwinkles into her mouth and started crunching down on them.

Our mouths dropped open; both of us watched her eat these indigestible pieces of shell. Both of us wanted to stop her, wanted to tell her, but it was too late. After a difficult swallow she smiled and said, "They taste pretty good. I like those, but I'm not interested in trying that black stuff. That dulse, you call it, looks awful."

Both Kye and I were horrified that we hadn't stopped her. We immediately dismissed ourselves. We left for the barracks area where we talked about the incident. Although on one side of the coin we found it all a bit funny. We didn't know the causal effects of eating periwinkle shells. We both swore no one must know about it, especially Jan. So silent we remained. I remember saying to him later, "We can never tell her the truth about the periwinkles!"

Sometime later, I confirmed that periwinkles were edible sea creatures. Even though that was true, eating the shells had never been recommended. To this day, I still feel guilty for having been part of that joke.

On the upside, in the days that followed, Jan hadn't suffered any ill effects from her crunchy experience. Additionally, Jan remained genuinely happy that we shared our prized periwinkles with her. Somehow this made the whole thing even worse for me.

CHAPTER 19

Moving On

MY STAY IN JASPER LASTED several fantastic months, stretching into about November of that same year. Autumn was the quiet time for Jasper. The snow began to fall daily. It was a time when the large numbers of tourists had disappeared. Animals, like the deer and elk came back into town to reclaim their status as the original owners of the National Park.

The locals also had time to take a breath and regroup. They had to get prepared for the next onslaught of a different type of tourist, the ski crowd. Their presence would bring a continuance of prosperity to Jasper.

I really noticed the eerie hush that engulfed the once bustling tourist haven. The contrast to the Jasper I had known during the summer months was astounding. After the many encounters in the summer, my time to leave had also come. I had been advised to report to my next posting, Fort McMurray. The temporary Red Serge duty had abruptly ended. There are many stories I could tell of female encounters that occurred while I was in Jasper. I'm not going to overwhelm the book with numerous similar accounts of that nature. These are stories of my police life and how I handled specific situation.

It still is with a heavy heart I remember Jasper at times. I had to leave what I regarded as Shangri-La! Everything was perfect for me. Jasper was an all-inclusive posting. It was the work, the adventures, the camaraderie, the locals, the weather, the wildlife, and the women.

I had fallen into real love for the first time in my life at Jasper. Unfortunately, we were never able to finish what we had started. We had but a few short weeks before she returned to Ontario to a previous boyfriend. He was a man I had never met.

Even so, I hated him, unjustly for taking her from me. In fairness, I must admit we were hundreds of miles apart where time and space faded our chances of continuing. I sometimes still regret my lack of action in removing the distance that stood as an impenetrable wall in our relationship. Over time we stopped communicating. We both moved on.

I forced my feelings of her love and beauty to the place of forgotten memories. Banished to that region where memories can only be reached in our dreams. Even so, her vision still haunts me from time to time, having left me wondering what could have happened if our relationship had continued?

CHAPTER 20

Go North Young Man!

AS YOU CAN PROBABLY GATHER, I was very happy in Jasper. I wanted it to go on forever, but one fateful day in early November the staff sergeant called me into his office. He had received a phone call from staffing. He presented me with a number to call. I promptly contacted the Edmonton Staffing branch, a Staff Sergeant Betts as I remember. The scenario went much like this.

I dialled the number reluctantly—took a breath—and after four rings I heard a female voice say, "Royal Canadian Mounted Police, Edmonton Staffing Branch, can I help you?"

I replied with a hesitant unsure voice not knowing what to really expect.

"Hello, I'm Constable Mitchell of Jasper detachment. I understand Staff Betts had left a message with Staff Johannes. He wished me to call him regarding a transfer."

The female voice answered politely and directly. In fact, she spoke without any concern at all. "That's right. Staff Sergeant Betts wants to know if you are ready to transfer to the Edmonton Guard Room for a six-month posting."

I went silent. The day had been made up of everything good, I should say, great! Kye and I had just received a commendation from the town of Jasper. The mayor, along with the main business community, presented us both with letters of commendation and a special Jasper silver coin for our contribution to their community.

The lack of transfer choice came as a complete surprise. I had some knowledge of the Guard Room and its activities. I got the lowdown directly from Tig's friend, Constable Sam Weis. He was the member who was in the accident with Tig while driving the lady to the Lloydminster Hospital.

Sam made it clear that the posting was used in Alberta generally as a "penalty posting." Officially the term doesn't exist; however, the connotation hovered over places like the Guard Room and Fort McMurray. Places neatly filled with members who had problems with the RCMP system or else had gotten into trouble somehow.

I remembered thinking, *why me? I hadn't had any problems! After all, didn't I just get a big thank-you from Jasper for a job well done?*

Of course, I couldn't tell Staff Betts' clerk that, but it upset me, nevertheless.

I said no and good day to the lady as politely as I could then hung up the phone. Staff Johannes could tell I was disappointed. He asked what the problem was, and I explained my take on spending six months' downtime guarding prisoners when I should be out doing real police work.

As usual he was supportive and understanding of my point of view.

He said, "I'll make a call to Staff Betts and arrange a staffing interview for you as soon as possible in person so you can explain your concerns."

I thanked him and really hoped my personal appearance before Staff Betts would produce some other possibilities. I was reminded by one of the corporals in the office of that old saying, "Be careful what you ask for, you may just get it!" I shrugged it off and remained hopeful of the personal interview with Staff Betts.

The meeting in Edmonton had been arranged for the next day. The appointment time was 2:30 p.m. I had approximately 208 miles to travel, so off I left in our unmarked police vehicle bright and early at 7:00 a.m. I arrived in Edmonton just in time to have a quick lunch and find the Edmonton Subdivision office.

I was quickly ushered into Staff Betts' office where I was motioned to sit down in the usual RCMP fashion—directly across from his desk. He seemed friendly enough. He was a seasoned member with years of experience convincing young members to accept undesirable transfers. I didn't respect his real talent back then. It wasn't until much later in my career that I came to realize the difficulties facing staffing officers when manning undesirable places like the Guard Room.

In a short half hour, Staff Betts got to know me a bit better. He asked me my aspirations in the Force and my personal background. He had me give the reasons why I didn't want to be transferred to the Guard Room.

I felt it necessary to be candid and very direct. "Staff, I come from New Brunswick, and for a long time I've wanted to be a policeman, especially a member of the Force. I vowed I'd never be a fake policeman!"

"What do you mean by that, Tim?"

I mean someone who doesn't work on the road—in a municipal or detachment role. Working in the Guard Room would be fine, and I'm not trying to be arrogant, but you and I know that a member can be very efficient at that job in two weeks. The rest of the six months would be nothing more than downtime. At least that's how I see it! Of course, I'll go anywhere the Force sees fit to post me, Staff. I know I'll not be very happy there."

"I see. Well, you need a transfer to somewhere challenging where you'll be busy right? So, you can learn a lot."

"Yes Sir."

"Well, what do you think of Fort McMurray?"

I suddenly realized I had been duped. My big mouth had just gotten me transferred to McMurray.

What could I say after in response to that? "Yes, Staff, I'd be happy to transfer there."

Within three hours I was back in Jasper where I was met by the afternoon steno. She had a piece of paper in her hand indicating I was transferred to Fort McMurray. It all suddenly sunk in. I was going north.

The day finally came to leave Jasper for the last time. I distinctly remember looking up at the heavy cloud cover on that frosty November morning. The vision seemed to echo my feelings of uncertainty of what was to come. I suddenly experienced the bittersweet feelings of excitement and regret. I had noticed the temperature had dropped severely as I travelled north. It had dropped into the sub-zero point by that time.

CHAPTER 21

Surprise Greetings

ABOUT A BLOCK OFF THE highway, I noticed a marked police car parked at the post office on my left. With a sense of relief, I pulled into the parking lot and went inside.

I saw a female member in uniform standing in line with a parcel in her hands. I walked directly up to her and introduced myself. I politely asked directions to the office.

She turned and looked at me as if I had two heads, then said very bluntly, "Can't you see I'm busy? I don't have time to give you directions!"

I was very tired, and the only thing on my mind was to unload my truck and sleep.

I couldn't help myself, so I answered just as abruptly as her response, "What! You can't give me simple directions to the office? What's the matter with you?"

I surprised myself. I had never treated another member of the Force like that before, especially in public. It just wasn't done out of mutual respect. She just glared at me without saying another word.

"Aren't you going to say anything, Constable?"

All the civilian patrons looked at us intently. They seemed to enjoy the impending confrontation. She maintained her silence, continuing to give me a glare that would make ice melt at the North Pole. I couldn't believe her reaction. I had been polite and only asked for simple directions to the office.

I turned and walked out of the building. I remember saying to myself out loud, "What a bitch! I sure hope this isn't a sign of how the other members are up here?"

"No, they're not!" One of the civilians from the post office had followed me outside.

"She is a bitch! I know of her, and others here say the same thing."

I didn't quite know what to say. He went on to introduce himself as the local Royal Bank manager. He offered to have me follow him to the RCMP office downtown on Franklin Avenue. I thanked him for his very kind help then jumped into my truck and followed.

Before long he had left me at the front of the Fort McMurray office. I stared at it in disbelief. It was nothing more than several modular type trailers fastened together to a brick covered garage, making it almost look like a real building.

I reminded myself that it was dark. I was tired. I needed some food, but most of all rest.

I walked through the front door and looked around at the cluttered makeshift office to see what I was up against. A very short Indigenous lady was sitting at her desk on the other side of the well-used, gouged, and otherwise scarred counter area. I had heard rumours of the Wild West lifestyle that I could expect while working in McMurray. That vision somehow supported those rumours.

The lady who met me at the front counter of the detachment was Mrs. Bradley, later known to us all as Mrs. B. Right away, she had no problem recognizing me as a member. I was made to feel welcome by her friendly demeanour. She had a very strong mothering instinct, so she could tell I was hungry and tired. She let me in and provided me with a sandwich that somehow magically appeared along with a hot cup of sweetened coffee.

I gulped down both without hesitation. All the while I was eating, she managed to get my name, presented me with my schedule, handled two phone calls, a front counter complaint and answered two member requests on the police radio. If I hadn't realized it then, I would later understand that Mrs. B. ran the detachment. Sure, we had a staff sergeant and even an officer in charge, but the most important person was Mrs. B. She knew everyone, good and bad. She was the "go to" person for geographic information, equipment, and especially when it came down to knowing "who was who in the zoo."

I spent four years in Fort McMurray. In my time there, I sometimes watched other members sell Mrs. B. short. Contrarily, I never did because I recognized her as a gem. She treated all of us like her sons and daughters, always looking out for our safety and reputations. I had watched her on many occasions as she verbally defended each of us against untrue allegations sometimes made by disgruntled drunks and bad guys. She even proved herself to be adept at intervening physically on our behalf when trouble erupted at the front counter. She was a fearless attribute of the Force in Fort McMurray. I respected her then and to the present day.

Getting back to my first night in For McMurray, Mrs. Bradley not only fed me but also arranged for another member to direct me to my sleeping accommodations. Unlike most detachments, the barracks were located about a block away in a separate building. He was directed to help me unload my belongings and to make sure I had everything I needed to get rested up for work the next day.

I settled down for the night at my new post in my new bed. My mind exploded with the visions of all that had happened to me during that one day: the hazardous trip, the encounter with the female member from hell, the kind civilian, and finally Mrs. B. Before I drifted off to sleep, I concluded that Fort McMurray was going to be an interesting and challenging place to work. I was excited at my new transfer.

I woke up early the next morning feeling stiff and slightly tired.

It had been a long hazardous trip.

Within minutes of putting on my uniform I felt as good as new. I decided to walk to the office. As I approached the top step, I stopped abruptly. A large jet-black raven stood in my path. It squawked and squawked while flapping its wings violently. I had never seen a raven up close before. Truthfully, I didn't know much about them. I wasn't too sure if it could hurt me or just make a lot of noise. It was something they hadn't trained us for at Depot. It acted like it had no fear. Even though I was almost twenty times larger, the raven stood its ground. There was only one thing I was sure about in that situation. The raven wasn't about to yield its position without some physical action on my part. My proximity allowed me to observe first-hand the pointy sharpness of its beak and the size of its sharp claws on its feet. I didn't move, and the raven didn't move from its loud offensive stance. We seemed to be in a Mexican standoff. I had a gun and could surely shoot the thing, and the raven had its natural ability to move like lightning with its sharp attributes.

In the seconds it had taken to try to solve my dilemma, I heard a car door slam behind me. I heard a voice say, "Have you got a problem?"

I didn't really want to turn to look for fear the raven would attack while I was off guard.

"Step back slowly, and I'll show you how to deal with our friend Chester there!"

I still hadn't turned around but did as the voice said. All the while the raven kept squawking and flapping its wings violently. When I reached the bottom step, I turned and there was the female member, the one from the post office. She was smiling and almost laughing. She pushed by me, grabbed the broom I hadn't noticed laying against the railing. She walked directly to the raven and with the brush end swept at it. The bird backed up then took flight away from the office.

She laid the broom against the building, then calmly said, "That's how you handle Chester."

I felt so embarrassed. A woman calmly sweeps a raven off the detachment steps like it was nothing. My only action had been to stand there shivering in my boots with thoughts of injury and death. To make things worse it was she—the bitch from the post office. My face was red, I was sure of it.

Then she spoke, "Don't just stand there! Come on in and have coffee, and I'll tell you all about Chester."

She smiled at me again, so I followed her inside.

She looked at Mrs. B. and said with a slight laugh, "Tim here has just met Chester. I'm not sure, but I think Chester might have won. Our new constable knows what to do now, I think?"

Mrs. B. said, "Good morning, Tim, I see you've met both Chester and Constable Corke here."

"Yes! I guess I have?"

"Follow her back to the coffee room and she'll tell you Chester's story. I'll come and get you when I finish making up your file. I'll possibly need some additional information."

"Okay." I was still a bit humbled over the incident and wondered if Fort McMurray was always going to be this strange. A woman who wouldn't even talk to me yesterday is now smiling and joking around with a great sense of humour. It seemed I had a lot to learn about the female psyche and the ravens of the north.

Once I made a coffee and sat down facing Dale, she stuck out her hand and formally introduced herself as Dale Corke.

"I'm sorry about last night. I can be a bitch sometimes! I was having a bad day, and I was tired—never talk to me when I'm tired. That's for your own good. Again, I'm sorry. Where are you from?"

"Do you mean where did I just come in from?"

"No, I know you were in Jasper with an easy touch of a job, working Red Serge duty, wasn't it?"

"Ya—Yes."

"Well, you'll have to earn your keep up here! We're all run off our feet! Everyone could work double shifts and we still wouldn't catch up! I'm carrying at least one hundred open files at any one time. Some of the guys have a lot more."

I said nothing in response. I thought even though this woman seems to be in a good mood she is still a bitch. Or she's the type that tells you just what she thinks without any kindness filters. I remember thinking, *I wonder how many guys she offends out there.*

I knew I would never like her, but I had to find a way to tolerate her. It was highly possible I might have to work with her. So, I politely changed the subject.

"What's the story about the raven, Chester, is it?"

"Oh! He's harmless! As long as I've been here anyway, Chester arrives on those steps at the first sign of snow. He can be found there every morning for about two months. He stands there squawking and threatening everyone each morning until we use the broom trick on him. The Indigenous people are afraid of him. They stopped coming to the office with complaints. It sounds stupid, but we all look forward to this time of year. The normally large volume of Indigenous nuisance complaints goes down drastically. This gives us a chance to complete some of our more serious investigations. Personally, I wish he were here all the time."

Just then Mrs. B. walked in. "Tim, it's customary for a new member of the detachment to ride along with someone that has been here for a while. The concept is that you can be shown how things work here for your first few shifts. We find it works well. You've been assigned to work with Constable Demming. He's a great guy! He's waiting for you up front now."

"Of course! I'll go see him right away!"

I excused myself to Constable Corke, and then walked up a flight of stairs to the front of the office. I was open to anything that would help me fit in as quickly as possible. I was very aware that McMurray was a whole new ball game. It seemed like another world. It was sure a far cry from Vermilion or Jasper.

CHAPTER 22

Life at the End of the Road

I SHOOK CONSTABLE DEMMING'S HAND as soon as we met. "Call me Claude!"

I automatically replied, "Call me Tim!"

The first shift started with Claude driving and showing me all the trouble spots in town. I was impressed. He treated me as a seasoned member with some intelligence. In that shift, we arrested seventeen drunks. Both he and I had struggled with ten of them to affect the arrests. My Depot training soon came back. I remembered how to place them in the back seat of the police car safely and without injury to anyone involved. In very short order I learned how to process a prisoner, the politeness required, the amount of force needed, the proper search procedures, and the paperwork involved to complete the whole process.

The next two-night shifts with Claude breezed by with more of the same. We arrested drunks and attended complaint after complaint. Each of us took turns being the principal investigator until on the third shift we acted as a well-oiled machine. We definitely hit it off. He was a hard worker and I prided myself on being much the same. Neither of us was afraid to answer the police radio to take another call.

He requested that I work with him again and again until three shifts extended into a month. The sergeant and staff sergeants were happy with our teaming up. Together we attended more calls than the rest of our shift put together. We were able to obtain a larger than usual solvency rate, so the shift supervisor was also very pleased with the team. The other four members of our shift started to fight for calls as we did. It was as if a competition had developed to see who could do the most work. It became a joy to come to work for all of us. It soon became known as the best shift to be on D shift.

The days were flying by. The life became very comfortable, and I was very happy. But all good things come to an end. I found myself trans-ferred to another municipal shift. The staff sergeant asked me to attend his office so he could explain the situation.

"Tim, sit down. You know that I'm very pleased how you and Claude have boosted the morale on your shift by setting the examples of hard work. You have both set a standard for the others on your shift. It has somehow motivated all of them to emulate you both. Everyone here knows that D shift is the best shift!"

I felt myself feeling proud and embarrassed at the same time. I never set out to gain recognition. I just had a great partner, so it all fell together. All the same, the staff sergeant's words made me feel very good.

He went on to explain, "You see, it's my job to make the other three shifts run the same way. When we have self-generators and motivators like you and Claude, we sometimes juggle them around into another shift. I'm sure I don't have to tell you we have a couple of members on A shift that aren't up to par. I'm counting on you to help those members by setting the same example you have for D Shift. It'll ease everybody's case load and make McMurray a better place—can you do that for me Tim?"

After returning to the streets on patrol my head had time to shrink back down to its original size, a mere 6-7/8 inches. Of course, the staff sergeant's words made me feel good.

Deep down I knew I hadn't a choice in the transfer, but part of me was very proud to help. Suddenly Claude and I found ourselves working opposite shifts. A year had quickly passed, and one day I had realized Claude's, and my shifts or days off hadn't matched—even once. Although I maintained my caseload, I found myself working alone most times. Despite making friends on the new shift, things never ever gelled. They were a group of individuals with a different dynamic than the D shift members.

The shift corporal was detached and aloof. He didn't seem to care if I was taking most of the calls or if Constable Blank was hiding out at the coffee shop. It was all completely different. They were friendly but not really *friends*.

The staff sergeant's experiment hadn't really worked in my case. The lazier members on A shift were still unmotivated. D shift was still the number one shift to be on. In retrospect, I think the staff sergeant hadn't taken the shift corporal's influence into consideration. That's why it failed.

During my tenure there, I had worked with many good members, male and female alike. We all knew why we were there. To work hard, catch the bad guys, and save the odd life if we could.

In some circles, Fort McMurray was regarded as being "at the end of the road." It was thought of as a frontier detachment where anything goes. I found we may have had a little leeway with uniform standards, but the potential danger and heavy caseload certainly made up for it.

The posting was truly disliked by the few lazy members working there. After the first year, I wasn't gullible anymore. I knew there were a lot worse places a member could be sent in Alberta to work. Putting all this heavy talk aside, me being single and thinking I was invincible, made the continual barrage of potentially dangerous complaints a lifestyle choice. A choice filled with adrenalin and outright fun which was further enhanced by every successful outcome.

Kung-Fu Walter

I WANT TO TELL YOU about an incident that just came to mind. It occurred back when I first arrived at Fort McMurray. Constable Leather and I were working a night shift together in town. My arrival had taken place only a week earlier. I had been working with Claude Demming, but he was away at court at his former detachment down south. I was still somewhat in the ride-a-long process as a member new to the detachment.

All was going smoothly until we came upon an intoxicated person.

"This guy's name is Walter. We pick him up four times a week in this condition. I want you to show me your arrest procedure completely, right up to booking him into cells. Go ahead you're on!"

The senior constable said nothing else as he stopped the car. I knew that he wanted to see how I approached the standing but wavering, intoxicated Walter.

The situation looked much like all the other arrests of drunks I made with Claude. The senior member remained in the car and silent with no advice. I don't know if it was a test or just stupidity on his part, neglecting to tell me about Walter.

Later, I was to find out that he was known as "Kung Fu Walter!"

I observed Walter staggering in a circle attempting to walk away. His curved path hadn't allowed him to really get anywhere. I watched as he staggered and floated in the middle of the road directly in front of our car's headlights. The lights made it very easy to see his every move. When I had gotten close to Kung Fu Walter, he mysteriously got his directional control back. He quickly began to walk away in a semi-straight line.

To get his attention, I yelled, "Stop!"

He surprisingly obeyed that command. I walked up to him and began to say he was under arrest when he jumped back into a fighting stance. His arms were drawn back with his fists cocked ready to strike. He mumbled something I couldn't make out.

He repeated it several times. As I strained my ears to make out what he was saying, it suddenly became clear.

He was saying, "I'm going to beat you to hell and then kick the shit out of you Mountie!"

I naturally took his statements and stance to indicate he was going down fighting. I delivered my reaction.

"You're under arrest for being intoxicated in public! Do you understand?"

I moved closer to take him into custody. As I moved, he moved, maintaining his fighting stance. He moved one way then the other way to avoid contact with me. The senior constable sat there without saying anything or moving in to assist me in any way. I knew from training that two members approaching an uncooperative was a better scenario. I was taught that doing that most times, no one would get injured in a confrontation.

I kept thinking, *why is Constable Leather not assisting me?*

Walter's movements were consistent with a person who wanted to fight. I repeatedly spoke to him, trying to get him to allow the arrest without an incident. I hadn't got any reaction other than Walter bouncing around with his fists in the air repeating his original threats.

The incident had dragged on for about five minutes by that time. To most people that may not seem long. Five minutes is a long time to have an altercation. Unlike in the movies, I wasn't prepared to let the bad guy hit me first. There was no honour in it nor was there such a code in letting the bad guy have the first shot. To add to the pressure, the senior constable, who still hadn't made a move to help me, seemed to be critiquing my performance.

In short order, I realized that my feeble attempts to talk him down weren't getting me anywhere. With one great lunge, I grabbed him and forced him to the ground. His arms were flailing, so I struck him three or four times to get him under control. Within the next few seconds, it was over. He laid there curled up in a ball.

From observing results of my action, I responded almost out loud to myself, "His resistance was non-existent—he hadn't really made any attempt to strike me with his upturned fists. He fell so easily—the flailing arms could have been out of fear—and now there he was curled up in a ball on the ground." I asked myself, "What was it? A joke?"

As those thoughts occurred, I quickly had pulled him to his feet. I simultaneously realized the senior constable was seemingly coming to Kung Fu Walter's defence. He grabbed me by the shoulder and issued an order for me to stop.

I angrily defended myself. I violently shrugged off his grip, making my intentions crystal clear. He would be next if he chose! I yelled back at the constable with words I don't remember. All I know for sure is that I was really ticked off at his late response. With a fresh load of adrenaline in my system I responded, "I wouldn't have had to fight with him If you would have helped with the arrest instead of sitting there with your hands in your pockets watching all the fun!"

He said nothing. He helped me grab Kung Fu Walter and gently place him into the back of the car.

When the back door was closed, Constable Leather said, "Sorry, I thought you knew who Kung Fu Walter was. He's harmless and only pretends to want to fight—he does it to all of us, but he never hits anyone."

"What were you thinking? How could you let me fight him if he is harmless?" I waited impatiently for more of an explanation, but I received the stunned look of silence.

I had always hated a silent response when questions were being asked. I just couldn't help myself, I had to say more. "You're responsible for him getting hit! I suppose this was all in fun? Thanks a lot!"

I slammed the passenger-side door after resuming my seat inside the police car. I distinctly remembering sitting there staring straight ahead with my anger. Try as I might, I couldn't make sense of the needless event that just went down.

I spouted one last sentence before we pulled into the booking area of the office.

"We have real confrontations and fights with individuals every day. I don't need to be tested with a phoney combatant! I've hurt Walter because of your foolishness."

When I think of it now, I guess I overreacted a bit too much, but he got the message. I should have been told about Kung Fu Walter before we approached him. After all, that was what the ride along was supposed to have been all about. Most of all, I was upset because I had hurt someone needlessly. Kung Fu Walter's face was swollen and bruised, especially his right eye. I had felt bad about hitting him so needlessly.

With the passage of time and the experience of the many other altercations I endured throughout my career, one would have thought that this incident should have faded into oblivion. It still stands out clearly in my mind along with a few exceptional others. Those were the special events that helped define for me which actions were right or wrong as a peace officer. I had always believed we were entrusted to do the right thing. On a lighter side, two good things came out of that incident. Kung Fu Walter never raised his hands at me again, and Constable Leather was always straight up with me after that as far as I could tell.

CHAPTER 24

Side Kick

IT WAS ONE WINTER NIGHT shift during my first couple of weeks on my own while working in town. I was halfway through the shift when I decided to gas up. I pulled into the Sunoco Service Station on Franklin Avenue. Before I could bring my car to a complete stop, I saw an intoxicated male leaving the business through the metal framed glass front doors. He seemed angry about something. Before I could get out of my vehicle, he appeared to purposely use more force than normal to slam the door. Consequently, his actions had shattered the glass in the door completely. He looked back, swearing, then proceeded to leave the area.

A service station clerk appeared almost immediately. He began to pursue the male to confront him about the damages. Before I could take any action, the suspect male turned to confront the clerk. He struck the unsuspecting clerk directly in the face knocking him down.

I quickly jumped from my vehicle to stop any further assault. Within a few moments, I had found myself face to face with the unknown male. He stood there silently after stopping abruptly when he realized who

I was. He was told he was under arrest for assault, wilful damage, and being intoxicated in a public place.

I laid my hands on his arm to effect the arrest. He exploded with his fists. He struck at me at that very instant I had touched his arm. He swung, I ducked. I swung back and connected with the side of his head. He swung and he connected. I felt the strength of his punch in the mid portion of my chest. I remember my exact thoughts at that moment. *This is enough! I've had enough pain!*

I grabbed him around the neck in a strangle hold, slowly dragging him toward the right rear of my police vehicle.

I did everything that I could to calm him down. I talked all the while to him, while he struggled to carry out a flailing assault to get free. He was very strong for being intoxicated. I was just barely able to keep him under control. It appeared there was very little difference in our individual physical strengths. The only difference I could see was he being intoxicated and I being sober.

When I got to the right rear side door, I had choked him a little harder to make him comply with my request. "Now just take it easy. I just want you to get into the back seat. Remember you're under arrest!'

He suddenly stopped struggling. He sputtered through the choke hold, "Yeah!'

"I'm not kidding. I'm going to keep choking you until you tell me everything will be all right! Are you going to co-operate?"

He gasped out, "Ya! Yes!"

Not being completely sure of his intentions, I released him very slowly.

"Don't try anything stupid! You are under arrest! Any further problems and you'll be looking at more charges. Do you understand?"

"Yeah!" He complied defiantly.

"All I want you to do is to stop fighting and to get into the back seat of my car."

Initially everything went fine. I had been able to open the door to the back seat while holding onto him. He reluctantly got into the back seat after a little more physical incentive. I wasn't about to give him any other choice. I quickly slammed the door and ran to the driver's door of the police vehicle before he had time to jump over the front seat. I had a real fear that he might escape through one of the front doors or even worse, drive my police car away on me.

I knew the vehicle I was using that evening wasn't equipped with a security screen known as a "silent patrolman." This was the protective window that normally separated the front and back seat areas of a police car. It prevented the person in custody from exiting the vehicle by jumping over the seat back to the front of the car. It also afforded protection for the driver from almost any type of injury a prisoner might intend to inflict. Unfortunately, that car was the only vehicle available for use that shift.

Because of my difficulty with getting the suspect into the back seat I hadn't been able to perform the proper transport procedures. Applying handcuffs to his hands behind his back then securing him with a seatbelt was the proper procedure in that situation.

The service station was only a few blocks from the office. Transporting him without the restraints would put me in jeopardy. As the possible scenarios ran through my head, I pondered whether I should attempt to drive away with my back to him. I kept my eyes glued to the rear-view mirror to anticipate any unfriendly actions. He was able to hit me from the rear, choke me, or even kick me while I was driving. I remained on guard to compensate for any threat. Contact with McMurray detachment indicated that no one else was available to assist.

The prisoner seemed to be calm and somewhat detached. He stared straight ahead saying nothing. I had just begun to drive when the calmness of the situation ceased.

He suddenly leaped forward grabbing my right shoulder and the back of my neck. He simultaneously yelled, "Let me the fuck out of here!"

As I had felt his hands on me, I knew I had to act quickly. I turned and got up on my knees on the front seat. I had reached back blocking his incessant blows. I returned several strikes back at him. The mutual bashing went on for what seemed to be a very long time. At the point, I felt that my energy level was about depleted. I made a last-ditch effort. I took a couple of blows to the face but I was able to grab his hair at the top and pull him forward bashing his head on the hard area of the seat back.

I became desperate to subdue him. He fought back with a vengeance. I was getting tired. I knew I had to step up the action if I was going to win.

I bashed and bashed, still he struggled, striking me in the head and neck. I distinctly remember the desperate feelings I had. The thought of losing the prisoner or losing the fight was not an option. With every ounce of inner power, I bashed and bashed until the events began to change. I felt his attack slowly weaken until that monument instant. A sense of relief filled my body when I observed blood spewing freely from his forehead. Suddenly it was all over. I shoved him back into his seat. He sat in a daze with blood still running down his face.

During the altercation, the Sunoco staff had watched my difficulty. They had called the detachment to get assistance for me. I can only imagine what the battle looked like.

My fellow members' response was a bit overwhelming, nevertheless a welcomed sight. It may seem foolish today, but my chest was filled with pride when I watched them arrive. Their emergency lights flashing, their tires squealing, and their sirens blasting out the universal warning, "Help is on the way!"

A more cynical person would have thought, *Murphy's Law was still alive and well! After the suspect was finally under control, back-up members had arrived on scene to assist.*

Instead, I gratefully thanked the members who had arrived to assist. Their actions left me with no doubt that I was privileged to be part of the family of the good men and women of the Force.

With their help, I was able to handcuff the suspect properly and transport him to the cells. One of the guys even followed me back to the office the two blocks to ensure no further problems were encountered.

The prisoner was booked in without any real problems. He didn't fight, but he was very proud. Mysteriously, he wanted to show us how strong he was by taking his right hand and ripping his shirt completely off in one swift movement. He casually passed it to the guard. He did the same with his belt. He pulled at it, while it was still connected through his pants, until it broke, rather than disconnecting as one would expect. He repeated this action with his watch and with his silver chained necklace.

We remained vigilant throughout this process until he had been tucked away nicely behind bars for the night.

Now, you may think that this is an ordinary event for a police person. I must agree that what I've told you up to now most likely happens to a peace officer somewhere every day. But let me go on with the rest of the story.

The next night when I arrived at work, I had found a note left to me by the watch NCO indicating that the suspect I had arrested last shift would be dropping in to speak to me during this coming shift. I wondered what this was about as no one had indicated or had noted on any of the documents in the file that this suspect was making a complaint against me for the action that I had taken during his arrest. So, I remained a bit puzzled until much later when I was called to the front counter of the detachment as my guest had arrived. Upon approach to the counter, I had made several observations of him. He almost didn't look like the same individual. I know that I hadn't told you what the suspect looked like during the incident but believe me, now this guy looked like a regular "Joe." Clean shaven, washed up, wide awake, polite, and aware of where he was at present.

He spoke first, "Are you Constable Mitchell?" I answered in the affirmative.

I asked, "Is everything okay?"

He indicated immediately that he had been very sorry for the way he had acted last evening, and he further indicated that he would like to make it up to me in some way.

I responded by saying, "You don't have to make anything up to me. Just don't fight with the police anymore when we're trying to arrest for an incident like you were involved in last night."

He said that he wanted to make up for it again, but finally gave up at my insistence. He left after a few more minutes of polite exchange. I never expected to see him again unless he pleaded "not guilty" in court for the charges that I laid against him. For a long while, I thought that what I've just said was true.

Until, one day, I had occasion to have to arrest ten Newfoundlanders that were drinking and carousing on a downtown street. The activity was almost normal in Fort McMurray in those days. Arresting ten individuals wasn't especially out of the ordinary either.

This group wasn't complying with my requests though; the next step would have to be a physical one. I called for back-up on my portable radio while the group of ten just laughed. Suddenly, like magic, the Sunoco window-breaking suspect arrived. He walked directly up to me and said, "Tim, which one of these guys do you want me to put in first?"

Speechless, I was startled at the offer. The group of ten was startled also. They must have thought that I was important, or that I was well known or something in the Fort. It was totally unusual for some citizen to just offer to fight with ten of them. Anyway, it worked, first two then five and finally the ten of them gave in without a fight. They all complied with all the instructions without one blow having to be struck.

After the incident, I thanked Dave for his help, as I had clearly remembered his name. This was only the beginning of a strange relationship. I didn't pay him, I didn't overlook anything that he might do, and I didn't even buy him a coffee. Not even once. But to be sure, it seemed that every time I was in this sort of bind, in and around Fort McMurray, Dave mysteriously showed up to act as my backup. During the following years in For McMurray, he had backed me up at least eight or nine different times. In all those incidents not one fist had been thrown in anger. I remember very clearly every incident ended with the suspects complying fully with my requests once he was on the scene.

CHAPTER 25

Cracking Rossey

I SOMEHOW GOT MYSELF INVOLVED with yet another incident that resulted in an unexpected outcome. I soon realized it would take a while to learn how to handle and process prisoners. It wasn't always straightforward. With humans, it's always a challenge. If I had the power to imagine all of the possible reactions, I would have enjoyed a reputation of being nothing short of psychic. It wasn't long before I realized that handling prisoners without incident was an art form.

About one month earlier, a new female member named Constable Trixie Roth had arrived one evening shift. I had formed the opinion from the very beginning she had the smarts and personality to perform the duty as well as any of us. I had been surprised on several occasions to observe her routinely wade into altercations when other members were being confronted or attacked. That facet of her personality would normally be an agreeable trait in a northern posting like Fort McMurray detachment.

But in the case, I'm about the recall, her normal course of action became a detriment in completing the task. When I think of the incident now, I guess I had never laid blame on her alone for anything that transpired. I had always taken the responsibility for what happened to Rossey. After all, I was the experienced member on-scene that evening.

In Fort McMurray, similar confrontations took place every shift. Most altercations came in one of two forms. It was either an all-out "donnybrook" or something as simple as just a "pushing or shoving match." It was the normal activity of everyday life in the Fort during those days. I did my utmost to adhere to that so important section regarding "the use of Force" in the Criminal Code. It states, "peace officer can use as much force as necessary to effect an arrest."

I never ever believed that hurting anyone just for the sake of it was the proper thing to do. I took the job seriously, so I stuck to the guidelines as close as possible. I know that the four years of experience in Fort McMurray had been invaluable. It provided me with endless incidents of decision-making opportunities that regularly tested my resolve. I noted on occasion some of them failed the "litmus test," but it was very rare and only on a small scale. Regardless of what others might have done when challenged or confronted, I remained adamant about my own use of force. Every day and every incident showed me with crystal clarity the correct response in any given situation. I routinely practiced the proper procedures using the initial control technique of verbal commands then escalating the amount of force accordingly. I strongly believed physical force was the last resort.

Anyway, I must continue the story of "Cracking Rossey." Both Trixie and I were working the streets of Fort McMurray that evening. We routinely picked up drunks in between attending to calls that were received from the dispatch operator.

The practice of routinely apprehending drunks was done for two main reasons only. It was for their personal safety and to prevent their involvement in any possible crime. The practice effectively reduced the number of thefts, sudden deaths, rapes, murders, and crime activities in general for us.

The whole incident began while Trixie and I were on a general patrol of the streets. I was driving up one of the main streets called Franklin Avenue. I noted a man staggering through the darkness in an unlighted portion of the roadway. It was about two blocks from the office. Only a small portion of his body was being illuminated by a distant streetlight. We had watched the male fall twice before we reached his location.

I felt he was drunk, so it was necessary to at least stop to assess the situation. I thought it was an opportunity for Trixie to gain valuable experience by directly taking part in the processes involved when arresting an intoxicated person. After all, it was the most common duty she would encounter while working on Fort McMurray Municipal detachment. All new members had to develop the confidence to be able to affect an arrest alone or with a partner. The two situations take different methodologies.

I pulled my police car up over the sidewalk to effectively block the male's path. After stopping about five feet from his location, I watched him maintain his movement towards us. He didn't stop until we heard the thud from his body as he contacted the rear car door. Trixie had gotten out first as she was on the passenger's side. When I walked around to assist, I found her standing against the side of the car holding the man up. He was quickly identified as a Mr. Rossey. I only knew his name and that he was some sort of local trapper and dog sled owner.

I observed the following symptoms: he had trouble standing, he exhibited a very strong odour of liquor on his breath, his eyes had a very glassy look, his pupils were dilated, and his speech was slurred and barely understandable. I easily confirmed my opinion that he was drunk. I knew that Rossey was single and lived alone. There was no one to call to take custody of him, so the decision was made to arrest him for being drunk in public. I also had knowledge that he had been mugged twice before while in that state of non-sobriety on the streets of Fort McMurray. Unless he demonstrated that something else was wrong or could assure me he had a safe place to go, he was destined to spend the night in the cells for his own safety.

Mr. Rossey and I found ourselves facing each other at the right rear door of my vehicle. Trixie was standing at the right front door behind him. I confirmed to Trixie that he was indeed drunk.

I was about to find out that Mr. Rossey had real strength even in his highly intoxicated state. He was a wilderness-type guy who had sled dogs, entered races, and trapped for a living.

After a kind of one-way conversation, I placed him under arrest. He said nothing, and when I opened the rear police car door, he silently refused to move or get in as requested. He stood rigidly with his arms braced against the side of the car. It was a form of resistance that some people utilized when arrested.

I put my hands on his shoulder and pushed moderately while ordering him to get in. In addition, I used the coaching technique, saying, "You won't be getting charged; we're only arresting you for being intoxicated in public. It's just to give you a warm place to sleep for the night. You'll be let out in the morning when you're sober, so get in."

He maintained his silence and resisted any movement towards the open rear door. If anything, he became more rigid by bracing himself, as if he were anticipating a harder push. Repeated requests resulted in no reaction. Therefore, I had to move to the next step. The normal procedure would have been to control him with a chokehold and make him place his feet in first so he couldn't kick us in the face while being placed in the back seat.

For some reason, I just pushed him a little harder first, after which he causally fell face forward onto the back seat with his legs still sticking out of the car. To prevent myself from being kicked, I grabbed his right foot and twisted it just enough to put a little pressure on it.

All the while I persisted with verbal commands, "Get in! Get into the car! Everything is going to be alright! Just get in!"

He didn't respond. He maintained a stiff stance while remaining lying face down on the back seat. I increased the pressure on his foot a little more. The results were unchanged. Extra pressure and repeated verbal commands were given to him. There was still no sound or sign of his complying with my request. I began to twist his foot just a little more when I simultaneously heard a groan, felt him slump on the seat, and heard the grinding sound of breaking bone. It had come so unexpected that I looked around to grasp for an explanation of how it could have happened.

In the darkness, I suddenly realized Mr. Rossey couldn't have moved his legs. In her attempt to help, Trixie had been holding the back-passenger door as tight as she could in the closed position. It effectively pinned

Mr. Rossey's legs in place. The only thing that puzzles me to this day is why Rossey hadn't given any verbal response to my repeated requests to get into the car.

I later confirmed that he was neither deaf nor mute. Immediately after I had gotten Trixie to release the door, Rossey pulled himself into the car and sat up promptly not saying a word. We proceeded to the office. He sort of limped into the booking area where he took off his coat and boots as well as surrendering all of the other appropriate items. I asked if he thought he needed a doctor.

He grunted, "No."

I looked down at his foot and it now appeared a bit puffy and larger than the other foot.

I said, "Are you sure? It might be broken."

He gave a negative response. Without any more fanfare, Trixie and I escorted him to a private cell instead of to the drunk tank. I didn't want him placed in a cell with others because I was concerned, he could have received more injury to his foot if an altercation were to break out between the inmates.

Because of my concern, I had purposely stayed past my shift that evening. I made sure to be present in the morning as the dayshift members released him. His foot had grown to twice its size. He reluctantly accepted my invitation to drive him to the hospital. Upon our arrival, he stubbornly indicated that he would take it from there.

I found out on the next shift that a bone in his foot *had* been broken after all. He hadn't complained or said a word about the incident to the Force. I expected to have to explain what had occurred to cause his injury, but he never said a word. I remember the feeling I had when I spotted him occasionally over the next month. Especially when I saw him walking around using crutches with a cast on his foot. Over the four years I was posted to Fort McMurray, the guilty feeling spawned by the part I had played in his injury returned each time I saw him.

CHAPTER 26

Mountie Runners

WHILE POSTED IN FORT MCMURRAY, I worked on municipal detachment, rural detachment, and highway patrol. One fall afternoon in my second year I was working highway patrol in a car alone. I had experience of about one hundred complaints under my belt by that time. I regarded highway patrol duties as a rest. It was a nice break from the consistently heavy caseload I carried on municipal duties.

Even though I loved the fast action in town, I enjoyed the freedom of highway patrol duties much better. It was composed of continuous complaints also, but there always seemed to be lots of time to create self-generated files. The list went on and on, impaired drivers, speeders, liquor offences, vehicle equipment violations, drug transportation and possession, stolen vehicles, and so on. Highway patrol duties taught me more about working alone than any other duty. It felt like my niche in life at the time.

I received a radio call from Mrs. B. She advised me to be on the lookout for a possible impaired driver travelling southbound from north of McMurray on Highway #63. It was a clear sunny day about 2:00 p.m.

The highway north of Fort McMurray had been graded in preparation for paving. The landmass of the area was muskeg. To counteract that type of unstable base, the highways were built with a greater depth of material to prevent heaving during times of freezing and thawing. Consequently, there was enough material to create a mound about six feet high. It had been piled up in the centre of the roadway. It essentially created a divided highway with deliberate breaks every kilometre to allow drivers to turn around.

I headed northbound to intercept any suspected impaired driver. A short distance into the mounded area I realized I couldn't clearly see the southbound traffic. I felt I would surely miss the impaired driver. I looked for somewhere to cross. It was my intention to sit and wait for the vehicle to reach my point. I spotted what could be an opening a short distance up the highway. The closer I got to the opening, the clearer I saw the suspected impaired driver's car. A blue, beat-up old Vega appeared to be twenty feet south of the opening.

I couldn't believe my eyes. I looked directly at the driver when I passed the vehicle to turn around. He looked totally oblivious to his predicament. I noted he was gripping the steering wheel staring straight ahead. After turning back into the southbound lanes, I stopped the police car behind the Chevy Vega.

I got out and stood for a moment in amazement. The impaired driver was still in his vehicle. The vehicle was running. All four wheels were suspended in mid-air with the rear tires spinning wildly. The driver had high-centred his car. I noted it had driven up the mound at a rather high rate of speed. Rocks and material had been sprayed outward on either side of the mound in a perfect "V" shaped pattern. The nearly twenty feet of travel along and up the mound without the use of the car's wheels was the obvious evidence.

It was certainly a sight to see—a beat-up, old, blue, two-door Chevy Vega with its four wheels suspended in mid-air. The rear wheels were turning at an enormous rate, spitting out intermittent amounts of rock and gravel creating dangerous high-speed projectiles. I knew I had to act quickly.

I hurried across the flying debris field at the rear of the car with one arm held up to protect my head and face. I was hit twice, once in my right lower leg and once in my right side. The rocks were small but stung, nevertheless. I climbed up the slippery gravel hill to the driver's side of the vehicle. I could see the driver was oblivious to his predicament. He was still gripping the steering wheel moving it back and forth as if he was driving. He was staring straight ahead, blurry-eyed, in a dazed state, with his head lowered slightly. I tapped on the drivers' side window. No reaction. I tapped harder the second time. The driver turned and looked at me. With a truly startled look on his face, he leaped from his seated position bumping his head on the roof liner of his car forcing him back into the seat. His reaction was one of sheer fright.

It was plain to me he was in no condition to open his window or follow any directions, so I had to take action to stop the car's rear wheels. I pulled the door open and yelled "Stop the car! Stop the car!" He looked at me without reacting. I had no other choice but to force my right leg into the car, effectively jamming on the brakes. I grabbed the gear selector and pushed it into park. The car's wheels were stopped, with the ignition turned off within seconds.

The driver was still stunned by my sudden appearance but was able to talk.

"How could you run that fast?"

I chuckled.

"It's the training —I guess!"

Somehow this guy thought that he had been whistling along the road fifty or sixty miles an hour. Suddenly, a Mountie shows up on foot to pull him over. The look on his face, his sincerity when he asked how I could run that fast, and his belief he was actually moving down the highway was almost more than I could stand. I wanted so much to fall on the ground and laugh.

I managed to compose myself and get down to the serious business of arresting the man for impaired driving, towing his car, and processing the file to its completion. When all was done, I told my workmates the whole story. We all had a great laugh. Someone had even suggested it was a good thing the media hadn't been present. He went on as if reading a newspaper story.

"Intoxicated male arrested on highway by local Mountie while on foot patrol. The capture was made with this season's high speed 'Mountie Runners'! Sources say they may be released to the public and in stores this coming spring!"

CHAPTER 27

El Cabong!

I WAS WORKING ALONE ON highway patrol on one of those cold winter nights with two feet of snow on the ground. Traffic had been very slow out there, so I dropped into town for a break in the calm. It was always busy so I knew something would jump out in front of me. I passed the Rivera Hotel and bar on Franklin Avenue. Then I remembered.

"This is the place something is always going down. I'll pull in here and check out what's going on out back in the dark!"

It was time to try my luck. I parked my car inconspicuously in the front parking lot. I began making a foot patrol around to the rear of the establishment to check things out. I walked over to the rear entrance of the bar. The only illumination that night was coming from the bar's open rear door.

My eyes weren't quite accustomed to the darkness. I stopped and waited until I could see more clearly. All I could make out were black figures of unrecognizable persons milling about. The sounds of music, yelling voices, and the loud outbursts of laughter presented a dangerous scene for a uniformed policeman to be attending alone. During those first few minutes the feeling of danger only heightened my interest. I knew I was in hazardous territory, so I moved closer to the lighted exit where more people were standing.

I had just finished speaking to a couple that were leaving. I wanted to ensure the intoxicated male part of the team would let his sober female friend drive away.

After checking several others without incident, an unknown male appeared whom I was to identify later as Jason Carlton. He was also known as "Fuds." That nickname should have been changed to "Thuds" after that evening's incident. He unknowingly approached me, possibly thinking I was just one of the other partiers. He was definitely under the influence in a big way. I stopped him.

"Are you about to drive?"

He peered at me through the darkness then answered in a deliberate voice trying to sound sober.

"What's it to ya? Are ya going to give me a ride? I don't have a car here—I'm on foot."

When he finally stopped in front of me, he recognized I was the police. He stiffened up immediately. With the lack of wind and the extreme coldness that night, specific odours were easily detected. During our short conversation, I had smelled the strong odour of marijuana.

"Have you any cannabis type drugs in your possession?"

I pointed my black metal flashlight at his face so his reaction could be observed. He was taken completely off guard by my question.

"Uh... No... I don't think so. No... I'm sure... No... No!"

His reply and his body language were sure signs my suspicions were correct. I immediately explained my grounds to search him. He froze dead in his tracks. I pointed my flashlight at the front of his opened winter coat. I caught the glint of something. I recognized it as the corner of a plastic baggy. It was the standard kitchen zip-lock baggy used to carry marijuana. In one quick movement, I reached into his coat. Before he could react, the baggy containing green plant-like material was in my possession. During a transaction of this type, I had learned to anticipate problems. To prevent any loss of the exhibit it was placed into my storm coat side pocket immediately to secure it.

I hadn't had grounds to ask for identification until that moment. Fuds had remained unknown to me, and he knew it.

"You are under arrest for possession of marijuana!"

I reached out to grab his arm or his coat collar area to complete the physical part of the arrest. I had been a second too slow. I watched as he swiftly bolted from the scene by running towards the field at the end of the bar parking lot.

The chase was on.

Up to that time, I hadn't lost a suspect during an arrest. My thoughts of his running away spurred me on to sprint as fast as I could. Nothing else mattered to me, I had to catch him.

Sudden feelings of desperation almost overwhelmed me when I realized I wasn't gaining on him. It was just the contrary, the gap was widening between us. In a moment, I knew I would lose him. He was just too fast, but there was no way I was going to let him get away.

We were both floating over the knee-deep snow of the field. I remember feeling my chest burning from sucking in the cold air. It hurt to the point I was about to give up the chase.

What can I do? He's leaving me in the dust!

My mind was burning with ideas. As a last-ditch effort to apprehend Fuds, I raised my left arm. Connected to that arm was the hand containing my black metal flashlight. Without any doubts at all I let the flashlight fly. It caught Fuds at the base of his neck. The contact knocked him to the ground immediately. He fell like a rock. Suddenly I found myself on top of him applying handcuffs. Then I dragged him to his feet. Once he was under control, I looked around hoping to retrieve my trusty partner. Luckily, its location was clearly marked. A few feet away I saw a stream of bright light proudly shining from beneath the snow.

Fuds wasn't hurt during the encounter. He was placed in the back of my car without any further resistance. On the way back to the office, I was able to have a civil conversation with him about what had just transpired.

Things didn't look so good for Fuds. I informed him that he was facing several charges: resisting arrest, attempting to escape lawful custody, and possession of a narcotic.

The night went on!

CHAPTER 28

The Role of Traffic Enforcement

HIGHWAY PATROL DUTIES WERE ALWAYS a great place for unusual events. I never knew what to expect during a shift. Tons of experience had been gained in the two years I worked on the highway. I had handled numerous injury and fatal traffic accidents along with having issued many weird and wonderful traffic charges.

In doing so I had been able to memorize the Highway Traffic Act. I had learned everything I could about moving violations as well as all the laws pertaining to vehicle equipment requirements. I really embraced highway patrol work. I found it exciting but comfortable. Traffic enforcement was self-generated work producing situations of choice. It was a freeing experience as those choices were mine alone to make. Working traffic duties also provided an enumerable volume of interactions with the public. It gave me great insight into human behaviour. The highway provided a place to learn how to control adverse situations by daily experimentation.

My regular routine was to drive using my radar in the moving mode. I used it to facilitate reasons to stop vehicles and write the appropriate charges to drivers or passenger whenever valid violations were encountered. Those included all manner of moving violations, vehicle equipment violations, liquor offences, etc.

The enforcement also covered everything from the infrequent infractions like possession of radar detectors, driving a motor vehicle while watching a television, or using purple fuel in an unauthorized vehicle.

My custom had been to work the entire length of my highway patrol area. That meant covering approximately one hundred miles of highway stretching from For McKay southbound to the House River. In the 1970s we most often worked alone. Whatever came up we just handled it. Hopefully explaining that will help you understand some of the stories to follow.

29

Nice Dress

I'M NOT ABOUT TO RECOUNT a story of death and destruction on the highway. Rather an incident that still brings a smile to my lips. On my twenty-third ticket of the day, I found myself at the southern extremity of our area, the House River. I knew where I was right away because of the large gravel pile on the left side of the highway. It had been stockpiled by road maintenance crews. It towered at least two stories above the ground. Traffic flow at that time of day was usually moderate. It was Tuesday, and there was no reason to expect any other result.

It was obvious the normal traffic flow was slowing at House River for some reason. My immediate thoughts were an accident must have occurred. I searched the ditches and roadway in both directions to find the reason for the reduced traffic flow. The normal speed of a hundred kilometres per hour had become forty kilometres per hour or less. The traffic was just crawling past the House River turnabout. For a second or two I became agitated at being unable to determine the cause.

I looked around, then up—I spotted her. A lone female caused the traffic problem. A naked woman was standing in clear view of everyone travelling southbound on Highway #63. She appeared to be posing near the top of the gravel pile. It wasn't until I got a bit closer that I could see a fully dressed male holding a camera and tripod. He was standing a short distance lower on the pile taking pictures of her. He was completely out of sight of the travelling public.

No one was complaining. But the activity was causing a hazard to the highway traffic. Drivers were stopping directly in their lanes; cars were honking then swerving dangerously around each other to get the best vantage point. It would be only a matter of time before a serious incident would develop. It was called "stunting" in Alberta. The basic definition was "Any activity that distracts, startles, or interferes with any other user of the roadway" was an offence.

It was distracting. It was unarguable. The lady had our attention, but traffic congestion on the highway was the real spectacle to see. I manoeuvred my vehicle off the road by parking at the bottom of the gravel pile. Three other cars had pulled in some time before my arrival. When I exited my car, the drivers moved on without hesitation. I approached the gravel pile slowly. I wanted to give both instigators enough time to clue into the situation by covering up and coming down. Instead, the woman kept on posing and the photographer kept on shooting with his camera. They both ignored me altogether.

A climb was necessary on my part. Near the top, I looked at the girl and young fellow and asked what now seems to be a stupid question.

"What are you doing?"

"She's a professional model and I'm a professional photographer. We're having a photo shoot!"

"You're not doing it here! Do you know that you are committing several offences by standing here nude? You are distracting and startling those drivers down there! You two surely don't want to be responsible for someone driving off the road! Do you?"

The arrogant guy looked straight at me with a glare.

"You can't charge us with anything! We're not driving, and we can't control what they do in their cars on the highway! It's not my responsibility!"

The woman immediately began to cover up. She knew normal people didn't speak to a member of the Royal Canadian Mounted Police like that.

I took a breath and gave a controlled answer.

"You're sadly mistaken! You can be charged for lewd behaviour in public under the Criminal Code as well as under the Traffic Act for stunting! I'm going to give you another minute to cover up and start down this hill before I arrest you both under the criminal code!"

"But you can't do that! We didn't think it would be a problem. We're in the middle of nowhere for God's sakes!"

"It's plain to me we're not in the middle of nowhere. Look down there! I see at least thirty cars—all with people in them—staring at you two! What's it going to be? Are you going to comply with my request, or do I arrest you?"

The model got dressed while I was still speaking. I watched her half walk and half slide down the hill towards their green station wagon. As I finished my last sentence, the photographer began carrying his camera and tripod down the hill to join her. I followed them down. Before they left, I stopped to say one more thing.

"I know you both probably think that taking a couple of photographs out here isn't serious and you'd be correct if it was just you two, but when you create a situation like that"—I pointed down at the long line of traffic slowly driving by the vision of the naked model. Those cars are being backed up for several kilometres. With every male driver and passenger being aroused by your presence it becomes a big thing. It's now a matter of injury or death you might say."

The male responded as he got into his car.

"Yes, Sir! I'm sorry I overreacted. I'm just a bit frustrated! Sorry!"

Once they were gone and the traffic volume thinned out, I looked around. I could see no one for miles. Maybe we *were* in the middle of nowhere? So, I said to myself out loud.

"But isn't the female form great?"

CHAPTER 30

Keyless Entry

BACK DURING MY FIRST YEAR on, I had recently been asked to take up rural duties. My work area was the Syncrude project. There was much work to be done there. but on occasion I'd stray back to the main highway and create an "Alberta Check-Stop" by myself. I had to remain close to my area, so I usually set up at the intersection of Highway #63 and the roadway entrance to the Syncrude project. A check-stop usually involved random vehicle stops from a stationary point. It was all encompassing. Drivers were checked for any criminal code offences, vehicle equipment violations, and any other criminal code or provincial violation. Most drivers have experienced at least one check-stop during their driving lifetime.

I had just started conducting the check-stop when I realized I hadn't brought a portable radio with me. I had always found them cumbersome, so I had intermittently neglected to carry them with me on patrol.

The evening weather was so nice. It was mid-summer at about 7:00 p.m. There was a light breeze making it very comfortable to be out and about. Our emergency equipment still consisted of a single rotating red light on the roof and an external siren mounted on the front hood of police cars.

I turned on my rotating beacon to notify the oncoming traffic and began the check-stop. Since my Vermilion days, I had been a stickler for locking my police car each time I got out. To counteract any problems, I routinely carried a second key to the vehicle.

Unfortunately, that shift I had to take a municipal car. The rural car I normally used was at the post garage getting a new transmission. I had exited my police car to begin flagging vehicles over. As a matter of my subconscious practice, the door lock was engaged. I walked behind my car and randomly selected vehicles to pull over to check. My check-stop was aimed at southbound vehicles only. I only wanted to examine the cars heading to Fort McMurray. I checked vehicle after vehicle, interacting with each vehicle's occupants. I was having a great time still unaware of my situation.

The check-stop operation went on for fifteen minutes. I was just about to shut it down when I found a car that had equipment problems. I determined the driver was in line for a violation ticket. I retrieved the male driver's particulars to charge him with an offence.

I casually walked back to my car to write the ticket. I grabbed my driver's side door handle. With a sudden jolt the handle stopped abruptly. Suddenly it became clear. I felt it deep down in my stomach. I had no portable radio nor had I a second key to get in. It was crystal clear I was stranded with no way of contacting the office for assistance.

I tried not to panic. I knew I had only one set of keys to the vehicle with me. Those were the ones hanging from the ignition locked tightly inside. I looked across to the other side of the car hoping one of the doors was unlocked. No such luck. I checked every window, but they were all rolled up tightly.

I knew I couldn't do anything about the traffic infraction, so I returned to the violator's car. I covered the problem by explaining that I was going to give him a warning for the problems instead of a ticket. By the look on his face, I was sure he understood my real predicament. With a straight face, he thanked me and drove off down the road. To add to my frustration over my stupidity, vehicles began to stop voluntarily without being directed to do so.

"Wow!" I said to myself, "Look at this! When I want them to stop, they won't and now look!"

I initially waved them on while I tried to think of a viable solution.

I decided to continue checking each vehicle under the authority of the "Alberta Check Stop Program" to solve my dilemma. After going through the motions of checking everything, I started asking each driver if they had a coat hanger in the vehicle before letting them drive away.

I went through that routine a couple of times without results. I concluded the method wasn't working. I was beginning to think I was in a real fix. The sun was going down. A feeling of desperation began to build in my psyche. By the time I had gotten to the fifth car, I skipped the check stop routine altogether.

"Listen, can you help me here? I've only got one set of keys to my car and I've locked them inside. Have you got a coat hanger I can use?

The man smiled then laughed—then he caught himself.

"Sorry Sir, I know it could happen to anyone. I'm sorry—I don't have one. Can I give you a ride?"

"No thanks, I must stay here with the car, thanks anyway."

"But maybe you can do me a favour? I need you to drop into the McMurray office and ask for Mrs. B. Let her know my location and get her to send someone out with a second set of keys for A44. Can you do that?"

"Sure, I can do that!"

With that he drove off down the road. I watched him looking at me in his side view mirror. He was still grinning from ear to ear.

Vehicle after vehicle pulled over continuously when they spotted the emergency lights.

Somehow, I had felt a bit like the sorcerer's apprentice in that Disney cartoon. The segment where the apprentice gave the wrong spell and the place started to flood, with buckets of water being multiplied and poured out everywhere, and everything completely out of control.

Vehicles kept stopping, and I kept waving the excess numbers of them on. I had stopped saying "This is an Alberta Check-Stop, and I need to see your licence, registration, and insurance please?" shortly after "smiley" had driven off. I began to speed up the process.

I approached each driver and asked one question without giving any other explanation.

"Do you have a coat hanger?"

All negative responses resulted in the driver being quickly waved on so I could speak to my next driver. It became an assembly line of moving vehicles. I asked the question, a momentary stop, and then on it went.

It was just less than forty miles to McMurray from that location, so I knew that the smiling driver I had explained things to would be at the office very soon. I began to have second thoughts about letting everyone know of my stupidity at the office.

I dared to hope.

If I can only come up with a coat hanger, there's a chance of getting back into my car before I became the latest joke at coffee.

At least it would only remain a joke until someone else pulled a bigger boner.

Realizing that, I moved up production, walking and almost running to each vehicle, asking the same direct question. Then without giving any further explanation I waved them on.

I had checked about ten cars when an old blue 1955 Chev pickup pulled into the check stop.

I asked the question. Without speaking a word, the man reached behind his seat and passed me an old wire coat hanger. I looked at him without saying a thank-you.

"You can go!"

He did as I directed, driving off towards Fort McMurray looking back at me from time to time with a strange look. As soon as he was out of sight, I began to tear the hanger apart forming it into a viable door opener. It took about two minutes before I heard that blissful sound of "Click!" In the meantime, traffic had thinned significantly. The drivers that had pulled in voluntarily soon realized it was not a check-stop when they saw me breaking into my own car. I could see each driver stop then take his turn pulling back out after I continued to ignore them.

I immediately thanked the powers that be. I had just been able to turn my emergency lights off after jumping into the front seat when I heard Mrs. B. calling on the police radio.

"Alpha forty-four McMurray!"

I answered, "Alpha forty-four, go ahead!"

"Constable Mitchell, we had a fellow come in to say that you were locked out of your car, and you need keys brought out to you. Are you locked out of your car?"

There was a pause on my part.

"Is the complainant still there?"

"No! He said he had to leave!"

I knowingly decided to give her the boldest answer.

"Mrs. B. I don't have a portable radio with me tonight, so if I was locked out of my car, I wouldn't be able to talk to you. I just finished a check-stop so it must be a joke! It's probably one of the people that I had stopped. He's probably just being funny. Everything here is fine thanks!"

Without skipping a beat, Mrs. B. answered, "10-4!"

She had accepted I must be right; the complaint was fraudulent. No one had ever known about me being locked out of the car. My practice from then on was to always carry a second set of keys with me. In future detachments when only one set of keys were available, I always made sure I had gotten a second set made at my own expense. An incident like that never happened to me again.

CHAPTER 31

Love at First Sight

THE UNEXPECTED THINGS THAT HAPPEN can never be fore-
told. On another very cold night I volunteered to work a town shift at
the operations Staff Sergeant's request. He wanted me to help indoc-
trinate another female member with the routine practices used in Fort
McMurray. The temperature was about forty-five below zero Fahrenheit.

She was completely new to the Force and just out of training. Her
name was Chloe Myers. I found her to be a pleasant enough member. She
seemed cooperative and eager to learn. I drove around town pointing
out pertinent places and the things to look for on municipal patrol. I had
spent time discussing the normal bar closing procedures and explained
where the best places to find impaired drivers were located.

She seemed to be getting along fine. I had several opportunities to
observe her interacting with complainants and violators alike. She
appeared to make the right choices every time. The incident began after
we were called to the Riviera Hotel Bar to arrest an unruly customer.
The Riviera was famous for not having real bouncers. The bar staff only

served drinks. The establishment relied on us to bounce the bad actors and the drunks.

Anyway, all had worked out. We arrested one individual physically. She assisted willingly and properly, somewhat impressing me. As the night wore on, I began to feel confident that she could handle herself without too much assistance from anyone.

I thought it was time to let her handle a case by arresting an intoxicated person from start to finish. That would include arresting him, searching him, booking him into cells, and finally, completing the paperwork. I also wanted to show her the humanitarian side of arresting an intoxicated person in sub-zero weather. The Fort had a lot of alcoholics that lived from hand to mouth on the street. There were also those individuals who came to town from an outlying reserve or oil company camp with some money to live it up. Eventually some of them would end up intoxicated and unconscious in the streets. Most often they could be found lying on the roadway itself. With the darkness, they became nothing more than a waiting target for some unwary driver.

At around 3:15 a.m. we came across Lenny Coutou, a well-known client of the Fort McMurray drunk tank. He was picked up for intoxication almost every night. I stopped in front of him where he was lying semi-conscious in the middle of a dark side street just off Franklin Avenue. My headlights illuminated the outline of his face and body. He was completely unconscious. Neither the noise from my car nor the headlights disturbed Lenny in any way. His reaction was consistent each time I dealt with Coutou. He was lying there face-up, motionless as if he was dead.

Before getting out of the car I explained the situation to her.

"See this man lying here in the middle of the road, with dark clothing on? He is completely unconscious. If we weren't paying attention, we could have run over him quite easily. We have had other drivers run over people in situation just like this one! Another reason to help these people is the temperature. It's about minus forty-five with the windchill. We are arresting him because he's drunk in public, but it's also to save his life. There is no other place for him to go right now!"

"Why not? Isn't there a drop-in centre? We have them in Toronto."

"There are no drop-in centres or other social assistance facilities in Fort McMurray. These people have no one to help. We are it! Some would let them die. I say we can help them survive—even if it's for only one more day!"

She sat there silently. I was sure she got the message.

"Chloe, what I want you to do is get Coutou up as if you're working alone. Arrest him for intoxication. Place him in the car and book him in at the office. I want you to complete the whole process by yourself. But remember, I'll be here if you need any assistance at all, so let's do it."

Chloe gave an enthusiastic affirmative response.

Please be assured, I hadn't tried to set up Chloe in any way when I asked her to take care of Lenny Coutou. Things sometime just happened.

I watched Chloe walk over to Lenny lying face-up on the roadway. I observed as the events unfolded. Apart from my flashlight, the intermittent flashing light from my emergency red and blue roof lights and the headlights from my car, it was almost dark. The blocking effect of us standing between the car and Lenny significantly reduced light our headlights produced. It left us in a partially visible surreal environment. Lenny's face was not visible to a person standing over him.

Before I could say anything or move in to help Chloe with the physical part of the arrest, she began to lift Lenny off the ground. She had straddled him without thinking. She quickly pulled him by the shoulders towards herself until they were face to face.

The position reminded me of something important. Everyone who had arrested Lenny before knew that his nose was constantly running into his mouth with that unforgettable green stuff.

At that moment, Chloe pulled Lenny completely to his feet. He opened his eyes to see this angel that appeared to be hugging him. He did the natural thing—he wrapped his arms around Chloe and gave her the biggest kiss he had ever given anyone before. Chloe reacted immediately. She shoved Lenny back with such force he once again was about the meet the pavement. She bent over, spitting and coughing. She was almost vomiting on the ground. I quickly caught Lenny before he had fallen completely backwards. Chloe continued to wipe the front of her face with her storm coat covered arm. I arrested him and placed him safely into the back seat of my car. I returned with a handful of napkins for Chloe.

"I'm so sorry! I had forgotten to tell you! He is always like that!"

I felt so bad. I had forgotten to warn her in advance.

Like I said, "You never knew what was about to unfold." She said nothing as we drove to the office. She just sat there continually wiping her face with a fist full of napkins I had given her.

I later found out Chloe never blamed me, but nevertheless it made me wonder if Chloe would ever arrest Lenny again.

CHAPTER 32

A Consequence of Training

I HAD GOTTEN MARRIED WHILE I was posted in Fort McMurray. My new wife had been working at a gas station when I met her. During the final years I had been posted there she moved from job to job to better herself and her wages. One of her best opportunities occurred when she began working at the local credit union as a bank teller. The first Christmas at the bank, we attended their holiday office party.

I was a little apprehensive at first. Everyone in Fort McMurray knew very well who I was and what I did for a living. I was one of only sixteen members posted there. In the 1970s mounted policemen were still revered in most circles. We stood out almost as a celebrity at functions. Most people still believed that Mounties were the best of the best, especially when it came to honesty, truth, and fairness.

The majority of those present fell into that category. Of course, there would always be a few shady individuals present who disliked the police. Those were the ones that posed politically incorrect questions and made bold off-colour statements to undermine the individual Mountie or the Force itself. As I predicted, that was the situation. I remained on guard and a bit uncomfortable with my surroundings during the early hours of the party. Gradually I was able to relax and enjoy the celebrations. I wanted nothing more than to fit in, at least for my wife's sake. After all she had to work there every day.

Most of us accepted that image as a challenge to meet and maintain every day throughout our individual careers. I was not any different than the others. I had no delusions. I certainly realized that I was only human, possessing both attributes and frailties. Even so, I aspired to make my lifestyle live up to the Force's image and reputation.

The people at that party were participants of that time's belief system. Consequently, everyone had been watching my every move. My behaviour was critical. I had known that whatever happened that evening would most likely affect my wife's future work.

I did my best to be very polite and quiet but attempted to look as friendly and relaxed as possible to everyone. During my early days in the RCMP, I tended to keep a close circle of true friends. They were all members of the Force. I had been burned by outsiders once or twice before in Vermilion and in Jasper. It took some years of experience before I had realized the folly of such isolating behaviour.

To recap, the party was going along fine. I still enjoyed myself interacting with my wife's coworkers. The meal and speech portions of the party had ended. It was time for a party game. There were approximately twenty-five males and females.

The party game that was completely unfamiliar to my wife and I was about to begin. No explanations of how to play were given to the group. Canned dance music suddenly started to play. The bank manager began the play. He walked over to an unrelated female. He grabbed her hands then placed them on the back of his hips indicating that she was to dance and walk as if in a Congo line with the male leading her. She followed his direction as they proceeded around the room in a serpentine movement until they danced out of the room heading for another destination. Within a few minutes, they had reappeared performing the same ritual dance.

Not knowing how the game was played, I naively though that it was just a group dance. Everyone watched the couple proceed to an unrelated male guest. The female behind the leader grabbed the new man just as she had been grabbed. The dance continued with the three participants until they disappeared out of the room as before.

Again, they returned dancing into the room, stopping at a random member of the opposite sex and repeating the process. As I observed the dance play out, I noted that everyone was enjoying the game immensely. It looked like fun, so I hadn't hesitated at all when I was picked to join the group by a good-looking young female bank employee.

I had willingly begun to dance at the end of the other eighteen participants that had preceded me. If I could have seen myself, I was probably grinning from ear to ear like the rest of the dance party. The group continued dancing in a continuous line of male to female connections until the leader, once again, continued out into the hallway and into another large room.

Once the complete dance line was inside the room the action suddenly stopped. I watched intently to see what was to come next. I had eagerly wanted to fit in with the group for my wife's sake, so I didn't want to make any mistakes.

To my surprise, the leader of the dance turned to the female behind him and gave her a delightful almost sinful kiss. I had watched as participants, in turn, kissed the member of the opposite sex standing behind them. The activity went on down the line with everyone faithfully kissing each other. At last, it had become my turn, so I prepared myself for the kiss. I had smiled as the attractive young lady turned and faced me with a smile of her own.

She began to lean her face into mine and I instinctively leaned slightly into hers. Then, without any warning, I felt the sudden sting of a full-handed slap across the face.

Stunned, I reacted subconsciously without any control over my actions at all. Due to my mental make-up and my training with the police, I reacted to violence in a different manner than most average people. Instantly, the young lady had been flipped around and a chokehold had been engaged before I was able to stop myself. As I regained control of my actions, I found that she was positioned almost unconscious and halfway to the floor. The same reaction brought about by my training had saved me on numerous occasions on the streets of Fort McMurray. Unfortunately, in that setting it had a totally destructive result.

The group was overwhelmingly appalled by my actions. I immediately lifted her back up to her feet. I watched as she stood choking and gasping for air. Her eyes fought back tears of pain at my reaction to this simple party game. I turned deep red with embarrassment.

"I'm so sorry! Please forgive me! It was just a reaction to the slap!"

I couldn't say anymore. I felt my face turn red with embarrassment. No one made a sound as I helplessly apologized to the girl. The whole group showed no sympathy towards my predicament at all. That included my wife. Even after we left the party, she hadn't understood why I reacted that way to a slap.

Understandably, we were never invited back to any of their social events again. I was glad, as I never wished to relive an experience like that again.

CHAPTER 33

At That Moment

THE INCIDENT THAT I'M ABOUT to describe was, in fact, my first highway fatal accident attendance at that posting. Although I had been to several different types of death calls, it hadn't prepared me for what occurred that day.

It was another early sunny summer morning. Life was good. I had just finished a wonderful breakfast with a girl that I had recently met. We thought we were in love, or at least, I did. I was in a positive place that morning. I was left feeling it would be a great day.

Once I got to the office, I loaded up my police car and began my shift. I headed north on Highway #63 to begin my regular traffic enforcement duties. When I was about four kilometres north, my radio suddenly summoned my attention.

Mrs. B. called my car's call sign.

"Charlie Thirty-Six (36) I need you to respond to an injury, possibly fatal, accident. It's approximately ten kilometres north. I've received several complaints in the past few minutes. One of the complainants was a witness. He believed about thirteen persons were injured and possibly one is dead. It's an accident between a southbound bus and a tractor-trailer unit that was hauling pipe to Syncrude. I'll dispatch as many ambulances as I can, Tim!"

The second highway patrol member wasn't on duty yet, so I responded immediately.

"McMurray Charlie Thirty-Six, ten-four I'm on route. Can you call Constable Buckner in early to assist and maybe get one of the rural guys to head up here also?"

Mrs. B. gave me further particulars. A witness that was still on-scene indicated a northbound semi-tractor unit carrying pieces of one foot in diameter pipe to the Syncrude project had a large piece of pipe sticking out on the left side of the truck. It extended into the oncoming lane. A southbound Majestic Insulator Company school bus had been transporting about fifteen workers back to the Fort at the conclusion of their twelve-hour shift.

The witness stated he narrowly missed being in the accident himself after he observed the piece of pipe contact the front left side of the bus.

He had said that the pipe was just at the window level when the vehicles had collided. This had effectively taken the driver's side windshield and all the left side windows out of the bus. He was sure at least thirteen persons were injured and maybe one person was dead as he was lying against one of the broken windows unconscious. Finally, Mrs. B. indicated she was sending more members from town detail to lend assistance.

Within two minutes I came upon the scene. It was a sight. Numerous people from the bus were lying on the ground along the southbound side ditch. Some were covered with blankets, and some had nothing to prevent the shock of the ordeal. I noticed several bystanders helping the injured in any way they could. One woman especially was continuing to administer first aid by applying bandages to several of the victims.

I spoke to her first. I determined she was an off-duty nurse from the Fort McMurray hospital. I quickly determined that eleven persons were lying down in the southbound ditch. They all suffered from various degrees of minor injuries ranging from cuts and bruises to signs of broken limbs and concussion. The flying metal and glass had taken its toll. Because everyone outside had already been cared for or comforted in some way, it had freed me up to gather some more information.

I was able to ascertain which individuals had been the drivers involved, along with each of their states of sobriety. Both drivers were alive and unhurt. No alcohol abuse had been involved. They were told to stay put. I would have to deal with the unconscious male in the bus first. The registered nurse approached me just as I finished with the drivers. She had given me a quick overall injury assessment. No one had any life-threatening injuries.

"And Sir! I think the man on the bus is dead. I couldn't find a pulse earlier. He was the first one I checked. Do you want me to show you where he is?"

"Yes! If you wouldn't mind."

"Okay! But I should tell you I only checked for his pulse once."

Her reasoning was that the many other injuries had to be triaged also to determine which persons should be worked on first. She indicated that I had arrived on scene before she had gotten back to him to re-assess his condition.

We had been talking on the ditch side of the bus near the front door. She pointed to a male who was motionless and partially out of view from our vantage point. I pulled the doors open a little more, then both the nurse and I stepped into the bus climbing up one step. I observed an open-eyed male sitting approximately halfway down the length of the bus on the left side. He was positioned with his head against the edge of what was once the base of the windowsill.

I had hesitated there for a moment to allow her to speak and to survey any possible danger due to the severe damage to the interior of the bus. In those few short seconds, we stood there, something strange began to happen.

I want to be sure to indicate again that it was a clear day with no visibility problems inside or outside the bus. I was wide-awake with a clear head and clear vision.

Both of our mouths dropped open as we stared directly at the unconscious male. The nurse was positioned directly beside me. She let out a slight gasp. At the very same time a haze, then a thicker white cloud, formed around his body. It looked like a bright white cloud or mist. Whatever it was or whatever it was called didn't matter to us at the time. I just know that it seemed to suddenly brighten slightly in a fixed state. In the next few seconds, it began to move upward maintaining its general shape until it faded into nothingness as it touched the interior roof of the bus. Neither of us moved nor said anything for the next long seconds. She was the first.

"Oh! I'd never seen that before!"

I instinctively replied, "Yeah, I never ever believed it really happened! I only heard stories. It is real! We do have a spirit and we do go somewhere after we die! Wow! No one will ever believe it!"

Both of us stood there motionless for some time. It may have been out of respect for what we had just witnessed. In retrospect, I suspect it was indeed that sense of awe coupled with a moderate bit of fear. The kind of fear brought about by a suspicion that other stories of the supernatural may also be true.

After a few more seconds, both of us automatically resumed our respective positions as caregiver and investigator. We stepped up into the bus and approached the male together. We confirmed that he had died. I could see a very large gash at the back of his head.

The nurse and I never met again during my time in Fort McMurray. Since the incident, I have remained positive that if we were to meet again, she would clearly recall the incident as readily as I do. The vision of the human spirit leaving a body is an unforgettable experience.

CHAPTER 34

The Fort McMurray Lie Detector

AGAIN, I WANT TO SAY in the1970s, especially in the northern areas, people tended to believe whatever the Mounties said, and that was a good thing. I can only speak for myself. I had practised telling the truth throughout my career to other members, citizens, and to criminals alike. It gave me good feelings and certainly didn't hurt my credibility either. Although I must qualify that statement by indicating that there were certain occasions when lying on purpose in police work was a must. I was referring to occasions such as having to lie to save a life or solve a crime when normal methods hadn't worked on a seasoned or habitual criminal.

Someone in the Force in McMurray had suggested a method of getting positive interrogation results while a suspect sat in the back of a police vehicle. Then, sometime during the early spring of 1976, I and another member had just picked up an Indigenous suspect in a child assault case. The allegations suggested the suspect, Dixon Tally, severely assaulted a baby boy while he was left in his care by a relative. It had been the second time his name had come up for a similar offence. We hadn't been able to find any witnesses nor evidence to the first offence. Everyone in the community was afraid of him, so no one would talk to us, with one exception—the victim's mother. She hadn't witnessed the assault, so we were limited in our evidence. Interviews at the office hadn't produced any positive results with the individual. We were game to try something innovative. Of course, we read him the police warning. He was made aware he didn't have to say anything and that he had the right to have a lawyer present before he did say something. He responded confidently to my reading of the police warning.

"I sure as hell don't need a lawyer! I didn't do nothing anyways, eh! You can ask me all the questions you want to Mountie!"

My partner went on to explain in a question to him.

"Do you mind if we don't go all the way back to the office to interview you then?"

"No!"

Since we were in Fort McKay, forty miles from our office in Fort McMurray, we surmised that he would readily agree. My partner looked at me to explain things.

"Dixon, there's really no need to return to the office. You see we have some new equipment now. Where you are sitting there in the back seat, we have the complete seat wired with a new type of lie detector."

I pointed out the entire area and specifically emphasized the exact area he was seated on. Dixon looked at me with a glare.

"Bullshit!"

"Look, why would we lie to you? Let me tell you how it works. You know that we both know your name, so after I turn it on and when the green light indicates it's ready, I'll ask you your name. You tell me that it's Bob, not Dixon. If the light turns red, then the detector tells me you're lying to us. Let's try it to prove it to you?"

I crossed my eyes and toes and waited for an answer.

"OK."

Dixon was familiar with our radio system. It was a little black box with two lights on it. One was green to indicate there was power to it. One was red, which only became illuminated when I depressed the microphone button to talk. I had previously informed McMurray dispatch that my radio would be off. I didn't want any other police car transmissions to interfere with our results, so I set the radio to an unused channel. When I explained the working of the lie detector I pointed to the radio as being the detector. It was situated within Dixon's view just below the front dash of the car.

Most people would know that this was our police radio, but he thought it was a lie detector. For the experiment to work I concealed the radio's microphone in my hand under the front seat. All I had to do was depress the microphone button to illuminate the red light.

After letting him think for a moment I posed the question to him.

"What is your name?

There was an unsure pause as I watched him stare directly at the radio.

"My name is Bob!"

Like magic the red light went on indicating that he had lied.

"I don't believe it, that's bullshit!"

I suggested another question should prove it worked beyond a doubt.

"This machine should be able to tell if you are married or not, so let's try that?"

"Okay"

"Are you married/"

He waited again, staring directly at the red light.

"No, I'm not married!"

We knew that he was lying so on went the red light again.

"See you are lying! So, see it's working fine!"

I looked directly at my partner as if this new equipment even surprised us by its accuracy. This was enough to convince him. He believed he was sitting on a lie detector.

We got right down to business; my partner took the notes and I asked the questions. Because he believed in the accuracy of the phantom back-seat lie detector, he confessed to the whole incident. The suspect had to go to the office after all to be charged and fingerprinted and given a court date. Some of you may think that this was ridiculous or absurd, but the court of the day was told of the whole set-up. They found him guilty of the assault against an innocent baby. It turned out the be a one-time deal. Word got out and I never had any other occasions to use that method again.

CHAPTER 35

Called Out to a Stabbing

ANOTHER SUMMER DAYSHIFT, A CONSTABLE named Barney Tourney and I volunteered to be on-call.

The duration would last from the conclusion of our shift until the next morning when a new set of members began their cycle of dayshifts. The normal member slated for that duty was away on an urgent personal matter. Being on-call meant that either of us could be called back into work to investigate a complaint if it was deemed urgent enough to attend.

On-call status was a voluntary unpaid function of the Mountie life back then. The voluntary part was arguable because there was no real way to refuse participation in the on-call procedure. Peer pressure assured its existence, as everyone took their turn at it. The hours of standing by waiting to be called were free, and the getting paid overtime wages began only after we arrived at the office.

After going to bed at 11:00 p.m. that evening, then being awakened by a call at 2:00 a.m. hadn't left us with much sleep. Every time I was called out to attend a complaint after hours, I convinced myself it was completely all right.

What the heck! I'm young and gung-ho. After all, I have nothing else to do but work!

I met with Barney at the office within fifteen minutes of the initial call. It was just enough time to pack a lunch and get dressed in my uniform. We had been notified that a man at the Syncrude project had been stabbed by an acquaintance in the same bunkhouse.

There was no information on his condition or whether the injury was life-threatening. While the Syncrude project was being built, mostly men, and some women, were housed in three different camps. Everyone was afforded a confined almost claustrophobic room measuring four feet by eight feet.

Approximately twenty-eight or more similar sized rooms could be found within each bunkhouse. The bunkhouses were nothing more than ATCO trailers strung out in rows. The same set-up was reproduced in North, South, and West camps housing approximately 8,000 workers or more.

People of every race and culture worked on the Syncrude project bringing with them their food choices, cultural habits, and unique beliefs about one another. It left at least the twenty-eight or more living every day in a close, unwanted environment.

The myriad of strange smells and interruptive noises was an inescapable factor of life that permeated each paper-thin wall. Privacy was at a premium at the best of times. To cope with working hard in all kinds of weather and temperatures while being isolated away from their real homes for long periods of time took very special individuals. Many times, tempers flared over misunderstood remarks caused by language barriers or by the social baggage of cultural discrimination.

I could only imagine the stress felt by each worker. Not only were they housed in what I called prison-cell-sized rooms, most were from other provinces and even from other countries. They were arbitrarily placed away from supportive loved ones, working in a foreign environment with strangers and crammed into a fox-hole-sized room. It was logical that some of them suffered from a "cabin fever" effect.

To broaden the envelope of concern, almost all the 8,000 lived under those exact conditions. Any members who were detailed to work the

Syncrude project were busy beyond belief. Numerous complaints of assaults, threats, and thefts filled each rural member's incoming complaint basket until each of us had at least one hundred outstanding investigations at any one time.

At times, I would find it overwhelming to realize that I couldn't possibly read all my files within a shift. So, working on the pettier complaints wasn't even a consideration. We all had learned to prioritize so the more serious complaints rose to the top. It was the only way we could best serve the public. That was why Barney and I so readily responded to the stabbing complaint call-out. We knew that a stabbing wasn't just another insignificant petty accusation we were so used to attending on rural.

Before leaving, both of us had rechecked all the equipment we expected might be required. Our practice was to always be prepared for the worst-case scenario. We considered and accepted the definite possibility the investigation would be lengthy. When heading north to the site, we purposely formulated a game plan. We had found in the past it made the whole procedure flow more smoothly.

The forty miles of distance went quickly due to the lack of traffic and the speed of the police car. Initially we pulled onto the on-site Bechtel Security office to gather more information. All we had garnered from dispatch indicated the injury wasn't life threatening, the victim's name, his room number, and the bunkhouse where the complainant was housed.

Aside from confirming the victim's location, Bechtel Security couldn't shed any more light on the case. It hadn't even been reported to them. We surmised the complainant had called our dispatch directly. Their security supervisor was a little upset with not being notified in advance of our attendance. Their practice had always been to provide protection and medical assistance right away to the employees. They had prided themselves on making every attempt to apprehend any persons involved in altercations and detaining them until our arrival.

The security supervisor happened to be working that early morning shift. He was an ex-member of the RCMP and had always been very cooperative with me in the past. He seemed eager to play an integral part in helping us investigate the alleged stabbing.

I understood his interest to be more directed at determining whether one of his own security personnel had been slacking off. Bechtel Security had a reputation for knowing everything that went on in the camps. It seemed to me the boss wanted to keep it that way.

I had always liked him. He had a strong work ethic that helped us really get along together. In view of the incident, he politely asked to tag along, but it felt more like he insisted being involved in the investigation of the alleged stabbing. Both Barney and I agreed.

The three of us had just exited the police car after reading the sign on Bunkhouse #45 in West camp. It didn't take long to locate room #26. I knocked on the victim's door. It opened immediately as if we were expected.

I spoke first.

"Are you Sylvain Penderkoff?"

"Yes!"

"Are you alright? Do you need a paramedic?"

"No, I guess I'm all right."

We were confused when we looked at him. He seemed perfectly fine with no signs of injury or blood on his clothing. I looked around the small room. I confirmed his room was undamaged with everything in its place without any signs of a struggle, blood, or a weapon. I was a bit bewildered, so I had to ask.

"You were stabbed? Where did the assault take place?"

"It happened down there!" He pointed directly down the lighted hallway.

"Exactly where was it? Can you show me?"

Mr. Penderkoff walked ahead of us several feet before stopping in front of room #18.

"It happened in the hallway right here!"

I took my flashlight and quickly looked at the floor, surrounding walls, and the outside surface of the suspect's door. I saw no signs of blood or any other type of visible evidence.

"What happened exactly?"

The victim took a deep breath then shivered somewhat before he began the story.

"I have a friend—or had a friend—here in room number 12. His name is Frank. He and I read a lot of books; he likes the same kind of subjects as I do."

He stopped talking and began to hesitate.

"Go on Sylvain!"

"Well, I had lent him my book of *War and Peace* two months ago. I came down here earlier this evening to get it back. He denied having it and he said that he had already returned it."

The victim stopped the story completely as if he had finished. I had to interrupt the long pause.

"Yes, and then what happened?"

His answer came in a wavering voice.

"I believed him at first, and then when I checked all my books, it wasn't there, so I knew he was lying! I went back to confront him. When he opened the door, I saw that he had it in his hand. He was writing in it. I sort of lost it and grabbed the book. He wouldn't let it go, and during the struggle—I don't know when or how, but that's when I felt a sharp pain. I let the book go and ran back to my room. Then I called you guys!"

When he had finished the story, he was almost in tears. I felt sorry for him.

"Where did he stab you?"

He stretched out his left hand, pointed to his thumb, specifically to a little black mark. I was caught by surprise. Bear in mind I was still very tired. I replied quite indignantly.

"This is your stab wound. A tiny black mark on your thumb?"

He was almost sobbing by then.

"I think it's a piece of lead from the pencil?"

"You were stabbed in the thumb, got a black mark, and you think it might be lead from a pencil? We responded here because we thought you were really stabbed with a weapon. A weapon like a knife or something!"

The incident had affected me strangely; on one hand I was relieved he hadn't been seriously hurt, but at the same time I was upset. By reporting it as a stabbing, such a trivial matter got us out of bed, then made us drive forty miles, and it turned out to be a pencil prick.

The Bechtel Security supervisor, being an ex-member could see I was about to say something I would regret. He quickly interjected.

"Look Sylvain! You are alright, aren't you? You don't need to have a Syncrude nurse or doctor look at your thumb, do you?"

"No, I guess not? It hurts though, Sir!"

"You know when something like this happens you should have called one of my security guys. They could have helped you with the injury and got your book back."

As I took the time to listen to the security supervisor, I realized his sensitive calm approach was exactly what the situation called for. I bit my lip and listened. He treated this guy with respect and compassion. His method of handling that type of situation was awe-inspiring for me. I decided then and there I wanted to treat all my future clients with respect and compassion even if they appeared to be a bit stupid. I convinced myself I had to be more vigilant when deciding what course of verbal interaction I would take, especially with victims.

Then, when he was finished talking to Sylvain, I added my two cents worth.

"He's right, when something like this happens, please call security first. That way you can get help with your problem right away instead of waiting for possibly hours for one of us to get here."

I watched as he nodded his head in agreement.

"So, if you're all right, let's knock on the door and get your book back from Frank!"

When Frank opened the door, he had the book in hand. Due to those paper-thin walls and doors, everyone in the bunkhouse had heard the complete melodrama. Frank readily apologized to Sylvain. All was well, and they seemed to be friends again.

The only unfortunate thing about the whole thing was that taxpayers had paid both Benson and I overtime wages to attend to the matter. Once refreshed the next day, I was able to laugh at the incident. I looked on the bright side, the file had been easy to conclude, and no one had really gotten hurt, unlike so many of my other call-outs.

The incident made me realize that being sensitive to a victim's needs was an integral part of the job. Part of me wanted to justify what I was going to say to Mr. Penderkoff by remembering that all I had done in the weeks leading up to the incident was to arrest and arrest. Everywhere I turned, I had people committing a crime or an offence of some sort. I was used to confrontation without compassion.

That simple incident made me promise myself I'd look in the mirror after work each day to see if I treated everyone right. It didn't matter if they were bad guys or good guys. It didn't matter because it was my job. Of course, I never literally looked in the mirror every night. It stood for the act of routinely checking how I treated people every day. Not obsessing about it, instead purposely staying aware of how I communicated with my coworkers and the public.

It was a work in progress, and it was a long time before I was able to perfect it to the point that it became a subconscious act. All I can tell you is I still had some rough days, made mistakes, and ruffled a few feathers on purpose and inadvertently on occasion.

CHAPTER 36

Will They Listen?

I HAD BEEN IN FORT MCMURRAY for about two years when this incident occurred. Another younger male recruit had recently started working on rural. His shift was over so he asked if he could tag along with me on highway patrol.

"It's okay with me but be advised that I'll be working the north stretch of highway between Fort McMurray and Fort McKay. I won't be coming south again after dark."

"No problem, Tim, I'm off tomorrow. I can sleep in if we're late." He grabbed his flashlight and quickly joined me in the front seat of C36, my favourite car.

For the first few hours we worked up and down the highway. Each of us took his turn checking vehicles or writing the specific infraction ticket that was required. It had been a warm, enjoyable summer night. We worked on and on until darkness set in at approximately 11:00 p.m. Both of us had had a fruitful shift with lots of liquor exhibits and traffic tickets. Since my shift was over at 2:00 a.m. we agreed that heading in early to process our exhibits before the end of the shift was a good idea.

As we were travelling southbound, I interrupted our progress by deciding to follow a single vehicle that had just passed us. I watched as it turned off at a service road. I knew the road led to a well-known gravel pit area. It was a popular drinking spot. I convinced my partner that one more liquor ticket or whatever would be great.

We turned across the highway into the east side road. It was pitch dark so we proceeded with caution, not wanting to run into another vehicle that may have been on the narrow stretch of road. As we rounded the last short curve before the normal gravel pit drinking area, we saw a lot of light.

Because of the warm evening, I was driving with the vehicle's window down. Without any notice, I heard the sound of many voices like that of a very large party. Before I had time to react, we had found ourselves parking in the middle of approximately one hundred young people. Most of them were sitting on all sides of the fire that lay directly in front of us. Some were staggering from group to group. Some were just lying asleep on the ground. The sounds of broken glass, intermittent yelling, and the ever-constant female giggle and shrieks of joy were intermingled with one giant gasp, then sudden silence. I was sure they had all noticed us at once.

I looked at my partner and I realized immediately he looked the same way I must have looked—pale and surprised. Neither of us had anticipated the large crowd. We both realized the situation wasn't good. Anyone who had been in that kind of situation, two against one hundred, would readily be able to identify with the ominous feeling of panic we suddenly endured. It was more than panic. It was a truly sickening feeling deep down in our stomachs.

The youths of Fort McMurray were generally pretty good to deal with on an individual basis or in very small house party groups. Our situation was altogether different. Neither of us had ever dealt with one hundred unruly, under-the-influence, bottle-carrying, and potentially rock-throwing youths fifteen miles away from any sort of back-up.

Ideas rushed through my head. How to bring the situation to a successful outcome was the only thing on my mind. The Mountie strength had kicked in. Right then I wouldn't say that we were afraid, but we were concerned with how to approach our dilemma.

We both realized that we couldn't back down. We were committed to uphold the law in any case and "come hell or high water," we had to follow through. We added to our pressure by thinking that all the members of Fort McMurray detachment had a reputation of being fearless. It was our duty to maintain that reputation. I don't know about the younger constable, but I was not known to run from a fight, and I was determined to maintain that reputation.

I looked at my partner and said, "Let me talk to them."

He gave me an implied affirmative as we exited our respective sides of the vehicle. The game was on!

The first thing I heard was someone yelling, "Stone the pigs!" then the sound of breaking glass. The crowd went deathly quiet as if they were waiting for our reaction. I remember very vividly thinking, *something bad is going to happen if we don't tread lightly here.* After all, we were outnumbered fifty to one.

For an endless moment, both of us remained motionless. All was silent but the crackling and spitting of the fire. In that short second or two, their eyes seemed to glow at us from the darkness like many demons in the night. Of course, it was solely due to the flickering campfire, but it only added to the stress of the moment. Many wild thoughts ran through my head of how I should handle our predicament. Even the consideration of using my gun to escape raced through my mind.

Somehow, I decided not to show any fear and speak right away as if our attendance was just another routine matter. I wanted to present the air of invincibility tempered with reason, especially to the troublemakers in the group.

I could hear myself say, "As all of you know, being here is an offence because most of you are drinking underage. I see open liquor everywhere. Now, no-one is saying that we want to arrest or charge everybody! But we certainly will if we must!"

I took a breath then continued after noticing that everyone was listening intently to what I was saying.

"We understand that McMurray hasn't got much as far as entertainment for people of your age. I sympathize with you, I don't really want to have to arrest or charge any of you—but most of you know me, I don't bluff! Remember there are sixty-five members stationed here at Fort McMurray!"

I paused on purpose to see the crowd's reaction. I continued after noting the silence.

"I can call them out in a matter of one click on this portable radio—maybe some of you might get away. But most of you will get caught, because I've already made note of at least fifty of you whose names I know. And of course, some of you will get hurt during this process!"

I took another breath, and they were still listening.

"So, what we're proposing to do is back out of here! This will give you time to gather your things, clean up the bottles, and give you a chance to get into your cars in an orderly fashion. Let only the sober ones drive."

Another breath then I went on. "Don't leave any beer or beer bottles at this site! I promise that this is not some kind of trap. We won't be waiting to stop you as you head back to McMurray. We know that you didn't come out here to get into trouble—we're going to leave now! I'll give you ten minutes to decide what you're going to do! It's totally up to you! If you decide to stay you all know what to expect!"

No one said a word; there was no sound except the crackling of the campfire. I turned immediately and walked back to the police car. Both my partner and I backed out slowly with our fingers, toes, and eyes crossed in the hopes that the reasoned approach would work.

I positioned my car south of the scene so we could leave safely if an unexpected turn of events resulted. We both looked at our watches. The first tense seven minutes went by with no sign of movement. The next three minutes seemed to be endless. The ten-minute mark was reached. Still, no one had left the gravel pit.

I said, "We'll give them five more minutes!"

We both looked at our watches as the fourteen minutes passed by. Suddenly a set of headlights appeared on the highway. Then we saw a second, then a third set until a string of headlights poured out of the campsite.

"They're doing it!" the young constable yelled out.

"Yes! They are!" I proudly said.

It was a wonderful parade of headlights streaming by us in a column. We were elated. At first, I counted twenty, then thirty-five, and finally we had watched forty-two vehicles pass our location. It was truly an uplifting experience for me. I thanked God and the power of being a Mountie for the peaceful outcome that night.

The blood returned to our faces as we watched the long line of red taillights drive southward out of sight. We both began to laugh.

"We actually pulled it off!" I looked at the young constable. He was speechless. I noted that he looked very tired, so I said, "We have to check the gravel pit first then I suggest we should call it a night!"

He nodded his head in agreement. I looked back to see that wonderful caravan of red lights once again, seeing nothing as they had already disappeared from sight.

We returned to the gravel pit to check its condition. Only five bottles were found, the fire was out, and no one had stayed for the fight. We were elated that the speech and our bravado had worked out. Our reputations were intact, no egos had to be bruised, and everyone had saved face. Best of all, the new guy had learned something, and I had learned something too. It was a great ending to a great night shift.

The Beauty of the Night

WHILE I WAS STILL ON municipal duties at The Fort, I had received a routine call one night. A suspicious vehicle was parked on a downtown back street. It was alleged by the complainant that the vehicle had been parked there for a long time. He had seen two occupants initially. Now there was only one, sitting in the driver's side. He gave Fort McMurray dispatch his opinion. He believed that the missing occupant was breaking into a nearby business.

He stated that the one in the vehicle was standing "six." Six is a word we all used to denote the position a suspect had taken when acting as a lookout while a crime was being committed. The complainant was well known to all of us. He was the Lebanese barber most of us went to for haircuts. He was regarded as a friend of the Force; thus, his information was regarded as valid.

I was in the vicinity and the only one available to attend the complaint. All other shift members were busy attending urgent calls of their own. That was not unusual as Fort McMurray was touted as one of the busiest municipal detachments in Canada at that time.

Luckily, the complainant had given the exact street location. I was able to park my car and approach the suspect's vehicle without giving myself away. It was a hot summer night. The area was very dark. The only light available was coming from Franklin Avenue, situated about a block away. The complainant had described the vehicle exactly. I noted it between the other parked cars without any problem.

I approached the vehicle from the rear. I observed the back of a lone male sitting in the driver's seat looking intently to the right. *I must formulate a plan* I thought. *I needed to catch both culprits.* As I got closer, I had decided that I would cautiously deal with the driver first, then handcuff him to his steering wheel. That action would free me up to pursue the other culprit.

I approached from the rear, moving from one vehicle to another until I had reached the objective. In one quick movement, I appeared on the driver's side of the suspect's vehicle. I positioned myself, standing just behind the driver's door. That gave me a vast advantage over the suspect. To see or talk to me, the suspect would have to twist his head all the way to the left in an uncomfortable position. That was a routine officer violator approach used to protect the officer from any overt action that might be taken.

I illuminated the driver with my flashlight. I confirmed it was a male. I noted that his window was rolled down and his vehicle was not running. As I pointed my flashlight to view the interior of the truck, he didn't move. As I had begun to speak to him, he listened. Within the few seconds of that encounter, I had made a startling observation.

The male was not alone. To my surprise and secret relief, it looked like the barber's concerns had been wrong. There before me was a vision of womanhood. I immediately recognized her as a local that I had often thought was very attractive. There she was, lying on her back completely naked, leaving absolutely nothing to the imagination.

I realized right away that she was embarrassed. But instead of jumping up and covering herself, she just laid there. She was frozen in that position, with her right arm placed over her eyes. I had often thought afterwards that she must have felt that if she couldn't see me, then I couldn't see her. I had spoken to the male youth about the situation.

He answered every question that I had fired at him. The only curious thing about the incident was that the girl was naked, and the guy was fully dressed. As uncomfortable as it may seem, I had a duty as a peace officer to protect a woman in that position. I had to determine that this situation wasn't a result of her having been threatened or coerced in any way. I knew that it would be embarrassing for her, but I had asked her to sit up so I could ask her just one question. I assured her she was safe and that no one could hurt her. After a few strained moments of communication, it was over. I politely left the couple with some advice on where to conduct that type of activity.

I drove off with a smile and the knowledge that no crime had been committed. From time to time, I encountered the woman while walking on the street. When passing her, I had always nodded and said nothing, and each time she had turned red. Little did she know, I hadn't told anyone else about the incident. Her secret was safe with me.

CHAPTER 38

The Antics of Constable "Bent Licence"

ON ANOTHER NIGHT IN MCMURRAY, sometime much later, a story unfolded that proved to me that it takes all kinds to do the job. The incident that I am about to relate concerns a constable that worked traffic duties. He had always performed his duty with a great amount of zeal.

Most of us believed that sometimes he went overboard. He routinely acted as if it was his personal highway. I came to that conclusion after observing his actions many times. A traffic violation was always taken as a personal affront to his character.

Thus, he was regarded as quite harsh when dealing with any type of violator, whether they were co-operative or not. It was true that he had a few quirks all right. For example, if a violator was stopped for a no-insurance charge or an expired licence plate charge, the constable always seized the vehicle and the licence plates as evidence for court.

To provide physical evidence for court it was routine to seize the licence plates from the vehicle. Most of us used a screwdriver to remove the plates in the normal manner.

The constable had never used that procedure. Instead, he would somehow bend the licence plate upward only once. Then he gave it a quick sharp pull downward. The plate would break away as if it was being held together by butter. He had done it consistently with little or no problem. I watched him remove plates in that manner numerous times. I had always been amazed at the ease at which it was done. It became his trademark.

I had tried to do it without success. Because he had performed the feat so often, he had come to be known as "Constable Bent Licence," or as most of us referred to him, just "Bent."

Bending ability and quirks aside, he was a very honest hard-worker who was not afraid to jump in to aid any of us at any time. It was just that his quest to perform his duties caused some strange events to occur at times.

One Saturday night, historically our busiest shift for calls, dispatch received a call from Constable Bent's wife about 1:30 a.m. I had just returned to the streets after processing an impaired driver. Suddenly, a general broadcast came over the radio for assistance.

Constable Best was holding someone at gunpoint in front of his residence. All available members rushed to the location. It was especially important for me, as I lived next door to Constable Bent. I was concerned that if Bent had to use his gun then my own family might have been in danger also.

My emergency driving response seemed to take forever although I was the first to arrive on-scene. As I approached Bent's residence area I slowed significantly. I stopped behind a blue, beat-up old Pontiac Firebird that was pointing at an unusual angle towards the curb. Evidence of a collision was evident on the right front corner of the car.

I exited my vehicle leaving my emergency lighting engaged. When I walked around the Firebird, Constable Bent and the culprit came into view. Bent was standing with his gun pointed at a male suspect who was lying face down on the roadway a few feet in front of the Pontiac.

I know that it was a serious scene, but before I reached Bent's position, I had to fight off the tendency to laugh out loud.

I was looking at a suspect's vehicle with damage and the captured suspect laying spread-eagled on the ground. Constable Bent was standing over the suspect, dressed in a white T-shirt with his Sam Brown gun belt strapped around his waist. The rest of the vision left very little to the imagination.

He was wearing a very thin, very short, pair of men's underwear, letting it all hang out you might say. Other assisting members began to arrive until we had about five cars with all their emergency lights flashing at once.

I put off the laughter to assist placing the intoxicated suspect into another member's car. He was taken away for a breath test to determine his sobriety.

Constable Bent remained standing there talking with the Corporal while other neighbours poured onto the street to see what was happening. Constable Bent, without any sign of embarrassment, continued to recall the whole event for the supervisor.

It seems that Constable Bent and his wife along with their newborn had gone to bed for the night. They were abruptly awakened by the sound of a vehicle colliding and the sounds of screeching tires. The noises had gone on for several minutes, at least enough time for Bent to get out of bed and strap his gun belt on. I heard him indicate he ran out of his residence just as the suspect vehicle was rounding the curve of the street for the third time. He attempted to wave the vehicle over without success. The vehicle drove around him and down the street.

At a point when he was just about to return to his residence to call in the licence plate number, the vehicle returned. Bent observed the car collide with every car parked on the shoulder of our street.

Constable Bent explained he stood directly in front of the oncoming car, pointed his gun directly at the driver and yelled, "Stop! Police!"

Bent said he was about to pull the trigger when the car stopped about two feet from his knees. He hadn't gone into any further detail, but somehow the suspect had ended up on the roadway face down in front of his vehicle.

The vision of Bent standing there in his underwear while wearing a gun belt still strikes my funny bone every time that I tell someone about those days. Now that's dedication!

CHAPTER 39

The Big Bang Theory

ONE EXTREMELY COLD DAY IN mid-January, I was asked by the rural N.C.O. to take a ride up to an area north of Fort McKay to pick up two members. Constable Bert Renoir and his passenger had been stranded due to a blown radiator hose. A truck wouldn't be available for several hours.

The N.C.O. was concerned about the safety of the members due to the minus fifty-two-degree Fahrenheit wind-chill factor. I readily agreed and began heading north. After about forty-five minutes of winter driving, I found them. Both were wearing full winter gear including regimental parkas, fur mitts, and mukluks. I noticed they were in good spirits when they climbed into my car.

I found them at a location where there wasn't ample space on the single lane road to turn around without going into the snow-filled ditch. The road was unploughed and narrow, with deep ditches. I didn't want to chance getting stuck, so I headed further north and hoped I would find a turn-around large enough to accommodate my police car.

I travelled approximately four more miles when steam started coming out of my car. I jumped out and opened the hood. My radiator hose had burst; it must have been the cold temperatures because that was what happened to Constable Renoir. Steam and water were pouring onto the ground. It left the three of us stranded.

I called McMurray to get help. I was advised that no one else was available until the night shift came on. We were told we were on our own. The N.C.O. said, "Take the nearest shelter and build a fire. Stay put to keep warm, we'll get to you as soon as we can!"

One of the other constables reminded me that there was a forestry station in the vicinity. He noted it should be located about a mile north of our position. We all knew that the station was always manned. It also came to mind that they usually had two vehicles available. We all decided we would walk to the forestry station.

Before my car had broken down, Constable Zepter, the second member, had been shivering since I picked them up. He kept saying he was so cold that he wanted to sit in front near the heater. Renoir seemed unsympathetic. Unfortunately, he remained relegated to the back seat. I wanted to keep us all warm, so I had turned the heater up full blast to accommodate him. Constable Renoir stated from the time their vehicle had broken down, Zepter had been continually whining about being cold.

It made no difference then. We had lost the use of both vehicles. In view of the circumstances, I advised Zepter to stay with my vehicle and use one of the emergency blankets to keep warm. I advised him we would return to pick him up with a borrowed forestry vehicle.

He would have nothing to do with that scenario, so the three of us started walking. We knew we had one and a half kilometres to go. A short time into our journey, I noticed how silent the frozen forest had become.

It was so cold that nothing at all was moving around. All the animals were snuggled down in their respective safe places to keep warm and conserve energy.

About eighteen minutes into the hike, I began to really notice the effects of the cold. I heard the eerie snapping sound that each of our footsteps made on the snow. Our parkas even reacted by emitting an additional noise each time we moved our arms. Even our speech had become noticeably slurred as we spoke. All of it suggested the initial signs of hypothermia.

The combined noises echoed ominously throughout the wooded area that surrounded us. The sounds meant we were alerting every other creature in the forest to our presence. Even so, the uncomfortable sense that we were alone out there overshadowed the event.

About that time, both Renoir and I noticed Zepter had dropped back behind us. He had fallen back about ten yards when I called to him, "Pick it up! We want to get there before darkness sets in. We don't know where it is exactly, so let's hurry up!"

He replied, "I don't think I can make it? I'm so cold my feet have gone numb, and I can't feel my fingers. It's getting hard to breathe!"

We both looked at him as if he was nuts. I snapped back, "We've only been out here for about twenty minutes now. I know it's cold, but we're dressed for it. Come on! Smarten up!"

He whined some more and finally said, "I can't go any further; I don't want to freeze so I might as well end it!"

Both Constable Renoir and I laughed without looking back at him. We stepped up the pace so we could call his bluff. I remembered thinking, "What a joke, what kind of Mountie was this? He must be a wimp!"

Then, without warning, Renoir and I stopped dead in our tracks. We heard the distinctive sound of a gunshot from a .38 calibre revolver. We both turned back to see what had happened. Zepter was lying on his back with his revolver still smoking in his hand. We both gasped. We both spotted the red liquid in the snow around his head. In that moment, it was horrifying.

"No! Did he shoot himself? He couldn't have?"

We were standing over him within seconds. He lay motionless with his eyes open staring straight at us. As I began to lean over to check him a little closer, he jumped up between us, laughing his head off. We had been caught completely by surprise.

The clown had staged the shooting by breaking two ketchup packets in the snow before he had lain down. We'd been had! Neither of us laughed. We turned and trudged on, not even looking back once until we located the forestry station. It wasn't until much later, about halfway home in the forestry truck before we honoured him with a laugh. He was quite a joker.

CHAPTER 40

Tea for Four

MY SUPERVISOR WHILE I PREFORMED rural detachment duties was Corporal Garde Schrill. He had a reputation for being fearless. He had fixed ideas about how to handle most things.

Sometimes his reactions to unplanned events were what I called O.T.S. It meant "Out There Somewhere." Even so, as an outdoorsman, he commanded respect. In the time that I had known him, he survived getting lost in sub-zero weather for seven days, he walked away from a helicopter crash, and survived several riot situations at Suncor during violent strike activities.

He was one of those members oblivious to his own frailties, believing he would always be unbeatable. He was the kind of guy who you either loved or hated, there was no in-between. He was also stubborn to a fault. That trait made it virtually impossible to argue a sensible solution to a problem once he made up his mind.

As usual, it was mid-summer during a hot spell. On that day, the corporal asked me if I would accompany him the next morning to do some small vessel regulations enforcement.

Without any hesitation, I agreed, not knowing fully what the duty entailed. He was sure to indicate we would be taking the detachment's jet boat up the Athabasca River some distance. He laughingly said, "Be prepared for a long day!"

He had given me a list of what to bring. His additional advice was to bone up on the small vessel regulations before our trip. I immediately began to prepare for the trip by packing and studying the regulations before the next morning shift.

Daylight had come much too soon. Although I had arrived at the office early to assist the corporal, I looked and felt like I'd been in a train wreck. I was tired to the bone.

Pretending I was wide awake and full of vinegar, I presented a loud positive greeting. "Can I help getting the equipment into the jet boat, Corporal Schrill?"

He turned and stared at me strangely.

"I did it all yesterday. Thought you'd know that?"

I remembered him distinctly going off shift the day before at the same time as I had left. He never indicated or mentioned that he wished me to return later to help with the preparations at all. Even so, I couldn't help but feel a bit guilty for not aiding him with all the equipment.

I finally concluded he had his quirks alright, but he was the boss. Over the remaining years, I was to bear witness to many of his bizarre ideas. I had always told myself, "I'll do anything he says as long as it's legal, and it doesn't endanger anyone's life, especially my own!"

On that first occasion, I hadn't known him that long. We were under-way shortly after re-checking the jet boat. Everyone on rural had warned me not to go, but it was too late. I had already agreed.

By the time that day was over I also found out Corporal Schrill believed the detachment jet boat was his personal watercraft. No one else was allowed to operate it whether they were qualified or not. The jet boat was the corporal's baby. He even kept it at his own residence hooked up to his own GMC four-by-four.

The good corporal thought the jet boat was the "cat's meow." He was amazed that a jet boat had no prop to catch on sandbars or to get entangled with debris or milfoil, etc. During the initial leg of the trip, he lectured me on how the boat could go anywhere. By the end of the day, he had done everything in his power to prove it to me too.

During the trip's entirety, I waded in the cold Athabasca water up to my waist and sometimes up to my mid-chest, to push the jet boat off the sandbars. Those being the ones Corporal Schrill believed he could traverse. When not doing that, we were stopping anyone afloat on a canoe, raft, or a plain piece of wood.

He explained our role was to check their equipment requirements listed in the small vessel regulations. I am referring to a bailing bucket, a whistle, and the dreaded second paddle.

I had prosecuted many persons for offences ranging from homicide down to littering. Each time, I tried my best to use common sense. On that day, I was detailed by Corporal Schrill to give out an endless number of detention orders to a lot of people. The order literally detained their boats from moving further until the noted equipment violations were remedied. It was a catch twenty-two scenario. I detained boats without a whistle, for not having a large enough bailing bucket, and for being quipped with only one oar. I enforced the small vessel regulations against all manner of craft. It didn't matter if it was a motorized canoe, a raft, a common paddle canoe, or a stick of wood with someone floating on it.

After the first twenty-five detention orders that I had given to people, I had ample time to have thoughts about the consequences. Setting the law aside for a minute, using my common sense, I had concluded it was wrong for us to proceed with the enforcement activity. I had come to the realization that the Indigenous peoples had been using the river systems of Alberta for hundreds of years, if not thousands of years, before we showed up with these laws. There were no overwhelming reports in recent Fort McMurray history that indicated large numbers of Indigenous people had perished on hot, calm summer days on the river when they hadn't had a whistle or an extra paddle.

I realized that the law was clear, but what about the individual peace officer's discretion? That was my discretion I was thinking about. Before I took any action, I had to ask that pertinent question. "Have the other members on rural been enforcing these regulations too?

"No, I think it's been a couple of years at least, maybe more."

Without saying another word, I made my decision. I began to give out verbal warnings instead of detention orders. The first time, Corporal Schrill said nothing. He sort of ignored it, if you will. By the fifth warning in a row Corporal Shrill looked at me a bit strangely. I knew he wanted to say something, so I felt the need to explain myself.

The corporal was a strong leader. He had never been prone to backing down. My first feeling was it might be a bad idea speaking my mind, but I plunged in anyway.

The exact conversation was fuzzy, so I'll paraphrase what happened. I explained that I felt we had done enough damage to our reputations with the Indigenous people. I stated we also relied on them for cooperation and information. In the whole scheme of things, I viewed giving out detention orders for whistles, oars, and bailing buckets pretty chintzy, compared to what might be solved if warnings were given out instead.

I hesitated but then explained, "I want to approach the affair in a way that can be beneficial for all parties involved. Why can't we do warnings from now on?"

Corporal Schrill listened.

"This would give them the impression we're bringing it to their attention because we cared whether one of them died out here on the river. What's wrong with presenting it that way? The way I just did with the last few warnings—stating these few items may save their lives or one of their children's lives while on the river?"

The Corporal just looked at me. After a long duration of uneasy silence, he stared me straight in the eyes and said directly, "That makes sense! Let's do that!"

Then, ignoring what he had just said, he abruptly changed the subject.

"We're almost there. There is someone that I want you to meet."

Surprised by his reaction, I looked around. I hadn't been able to see any person, building, or animal in sight. The look on my face must have given my confusion away. He confidently pointed to the east side of the river at something shiny. At first it was just a glint of light through the trees. The closer we got the more I saw. It was some type of shack. It looked about four feet tall and about six feet square.

"What is that?"

BEFORE MY MEMORY FADES

"It's why we came up here!"

"Does someone live there?"

"Oh yes! He and his wife have lived there since 1970, maybe longer."

"It looks like no water, no heat, and no windows?"

"That's right!" Corporal Schrill seemed very proud of their spartan living conditions, like he envied them.

When he pulled in close to shore, I jumped out to secure the boat. I waited beside the boat to follow Corporal Schrill's lead. I noticed he was carrying a small paper bag in his left hand. I wanted to ask him what it was, but before I could, he gave out a yell. A short, bearded man suddenly appeared. He returned the greeting by saying, "Come on up the hill!" We did as invited. Corporal Schrill hugged the man with a warm embrace. The kind one only gives to close friends and relatives. The short man stared at me as he released himself from Schrill's embrace.

"Who's this, a new recruit?"

"No, Tim has been with us for a few years now. He works on rural with me!"

Corporal Schrill went on to introduce me properly to Pete Fontaine and his common-law wife, Sadie. She was an Indigenous lady from the Chipewyan Tribe. I had been taught the Chipewyan were known as "People of the barrens."

They actually called themselves the Denésoliné (pronounced Den-a-sooth-leh-a), part of the Dené people of Canada.

Pete could see I was intrigued by their makeshift home. He satisfied my interest by telling me how he came to get the materials to build it.

"One of the first seismic crews that came up here in 1966 or '67 abandoned these pieces of corrugated steel, so I rescued them from nature. I used whatever I could find, things like those bolts, and then put it together like you see there."

To describe the shelter, I would say it was not more than five pieces of corrugated steel held together with a mishmash of bolts, sticks and discarded clothing. It had large patches of rusted metal where water must have pooled many times in its life as a home. Large areas of black staining on the roof had been brought about by Pete's use of the natural tar sands. He told us he tried to coat the severely bowed flat roof every year with the stuff. It wasn't pretty, but it kept them dry. There were no windows in the place and no door. They used an old warped weatherworn sheet of plywood Pete had found as a door. It would be propped up against the opening from the inside when protection from animals or bad weather was required.

At that moment, numerous questions loomed through my head. I wanted them answered, but I bit my tongue to stop from blurting them out. I remained polite, ignoring my need to know.

Corporal Schrill proudly went on explaining Pete's history to me. Pete and Sadie listening patiently without saying a word.

Pete had come from Quebec, where he, as a trapper, met Sadie at Fort Chipewyan and fell in love. They moved down closer to Fort McKay because Sadie had a sister there. He said they lived from day to day, hand to mouth, a hard and trying existence. In our conversation, I was quite surprised that the trapper was coming up to only forty years old. I thought he had looked closer to sixty.

I remember thinking, "What a hard life they must have, living here winter and summer in their four walls of corrugated steel."

Our good hosts suddenly interrupted us and invited us to stay for tea. On our behalf, the corporal readily accepted. Both of us had to duck down and half bend over to stand inside their home. It was especially hard on the corporal as he stood over six feet three inches.

Once inside, I had been able to clearly realize how cramped the quarters were and how spartan their lives must have been. From my observations, there was no source of heat visible, the floor space consisted of six feet by six feet. That is thirty-six square feet, just a bit bigger than the box area of a pickup truck. In addition, a table almost the size of the floor space was standing in the middle of the shack. Two crumpled sleeping bags were noted on the earthen floor. There wasn't any refrigerator.

The tabletop served as the only cupboard. I saw two plates, several dirty eating utensils, two hunting knives, a teapot, a half-eaten meal, a container of milk, and four mugs on the table. At that point, I wanted to leave. The situation seemed untenable to me, but I was compelled to follow my corporal's lead. I was positive he wouldn't insult our hosts. I guess I was in for a penny and in for a pound.

Sadie brought some hot water from a campfire that was outside some distance away. She began to pour a small amount of hot water in the mugs. She swished the water around in them as a method to clean them for our use. After a few short movements, I was given a mug with black tea already poured into it. I held it waiting for the others to drink first. When I came time to drinking the mixture, I drank from the cup with the same confidence as my corporal had displayed.

As we sipped our tea the corporal opened up the bag he had brought. He presented his gift still standing half bent over that disgusting table. I felt uneasy with a pang of embarrassment.

The thought had never crossed my mind to bring a gift of some sort. Even though I hadn't been informed that we might visit someone during the trip, I still felt guilty. As the corporal presented our hosts with a bag of oatmeal and two tins of coffee, I couldn't help but apologize to Pete and Sadie for not bringing something. Then I realized I had brought along a boot knife I had received from my father years earlier. I stopped apologizing.

"I may just have something for you?" I stared directly at Pete.

I reached down my left leg pulling the sheath and knife out of my boot. I presented it to Pete as my gift. His eyes gleamed as his hand closed over the knife.

"I had just broken mine two days ago while skinning out that buck over there." He pointed to a deer half skinned but hanging by its antlers from a tree about ten metres away.

The Corporal looked at me with surprise but said nothing.

I hoped secretly there wouldn't be a next time. I don't have to explain the reasons why I wouldn't want to travel that distance to drink tea from a kindly couple who served their tea from a dirty mug. Later, the corporal claimed it was an integral part of my duty as a Mountie. I somehow never came to believe that wholeheartedly.

An hour had passed by the time we said our good-byes. I pushed the boat out a short distance then waded out and climbed back in. The boat was pointed south for the trip back to Fort McMurray. The corporal remained chatty telling me other stories of how he had first met Pete and about the fight with wolves he had one winter, losing a finger in the process. I could tell that the corporal loved the idea of roughing it and the pioneer life. He admired the survival of the fittest principle and all of that. He confirmed it just by the way his eyes lit up when he told those stories. The whole trip back we didn't stop another Indigenous person in a canoe, raft, or piece of wood. It was very late in the afternoon when we arrived at the detachment office. I was exhausted. Before leaving for the barracks, I was surprised again, when the corporal commended me on my tenacity regarding the way I had handled the small vessel regulations.

"A good use of common sense," he stated, as if he was a proud father. He went further, thanking me for all the work of getting us off the sandbars and so on. Before he had left for the day, I had quite a swelled head. I felt very proud that I could impress someone like the corporal.

To reiterate, I said earlier that I had always thought the corporal was "O.T.S." That view hadn't changed but it was sure nice to be liked as a member by him.

The warnings that I gave that day paid off a short time later. One of the Cree men we had stopped on the river was Bobby Desjarlais from Fort McKay. I had given a verbal warning instead of a detention order. He didn't have a bailing bucket or a whistle. When he showed up at the office two days later, he asked to speak to me privately regarding some information.

I ushered him into an available interview room. I shut the door.

"Bobby what's wrong?"

"Nothing, Constable Tim. I appreciate what you did for me the other day, most Mounties would of just charged me like your corporal has before."

I answered with a question, "Did the corporal charge you with using a canoe on the river without the proper equipment before?"

Bobby quickly answered back, "No, it was when I hit my brother with a piece of wood some years back."

"What did you want to tell me?"

"I don't want anyone else to know what I'm telling you! Do we have a deal?"

"Yes, Bobby you can go ahead, no one will know except you and me!"

"You know Faron Javier's boat that's gone missing about two weeks ago? I know who has it. I'm pretty sure Arsen Powder had stolen it! The boat should be in the back of John Tremblay's house in Fort McKay under a blue tarp. I saw it there yesterday. Don't tell anybody that you got it from me, eh."

I thanked him and assured him no one would know where I got the information. He shook my hand and left the office as quickly as he had arrived.

I know it's customary to take a statement from a witness in these matters, but in the Fort back then, normal procedures were not always followed. In an act to protect my sources, I put it down as information received from an unknown informant. That seemed to satisfy my boss at the time.

I called a Justice of the Peace in and swore out information to lay a charge. He readily granted me a search warrant to attend John Tremblay's residence to search and seize the boat. That same night, another constable, Claude, and I attended to the suspect's residence to execute the warrant.

Luckily for me, John Tremblay was at home and the boat was still under that tarp. His arrest was uneventful with the whole file being neatly wrapped up within the same shift.

More than ever, I came to believe that the skilful use of individual peace officer's discretion should be added to the other variety of ways to solve a crime.

CHAPTER 41

A Door and a Tumble

AT LAST, A PLEASANT CHANGE. I was working with a partner. His name happened to be Gus Forzani. For the second day in a row, we were working north rural duties between Fort McKay and the Syncrude project. We had previously worked numerous times on municipal together, so we knew each other's idiosyncrasies. Our police approach was basically the same, so our work habits meshed like two book-ends. Our idea was to do the job but keep everybody as calm and cool as possible.

The day before, we had taken time to do some highway patrol type work by checking random vehicles for purple fuel, insurance particulars, licence plate validations, and liquor possession offences. Near to the end of the shift we had stopped a white male driving a motorcycle, by the last name of Champagne. From initial contact, he portrayed an arrogant and unbending nature. He barely complied with our requests to present his operator's licence, insurance, and registration. We remained polite throughout the transaction. Unfortunately, he wholeheartedly believed he was "at the end of the road" as far as normal rules of law went. He saw no reason to get insurance up at a location like For McMurray.

He immediately attacked our role as police persons. "I'm just driving in the country! You have no right to stop me, I can go wherever I want!"

"In Alberta, all vehicles driving on the highways or roadways must have insurance! It's for your protection and for the protection of other users!" Gus went on to explain the monetary penalty for driving a vehicle without insurance. Mr. Champagne indignantly spit on the ground.

"Fuck Alberta and you too!"

Gus went calmly forward. He explained that insurance is to protect everyone, not just you and your machine. When a mishap occurs, it protects the other car or driver that you may hit, even on the rural roads.

He resisted all logic. I interfered and tried my hand at making Mr. Champagne understand.

"It's as plain as this! If you won't or can't produce valid insurance right now, you'll be charged with operating a motor vehicle without insurance! DO you understand?"

"So what?"

That's when he became even more indignant.

I completed a traffic ticket summons for no insurance. It was in the set amount of four hundred dollars. I also informed him that we could seize his vehicle to prevent a continuance of the offence. But staying with our policy, Gus and I didn't want to escalate the incident. I continued with what we wanted him to do about his uninsured motorcycle.

"We are allowing you to arrange to have it pushed, towed, or trucked back to the West Camp parking lot where it will stay. Get it insured! Don't drive it again until you get the problem fixed! That's where you are staying while you're working for Syncrude, right?"

He remained completely ignorant even though we were trying to save him from losing his bike. Just because he was belligerent, we felt we didn't have to respond that way. We left him standing beside his bike hoping he would comply with our request. We drove southbound slowly working our way back to McMurray.

Gus and I had just arrived back in the area with a trunk full of files of incidents at Syncrude. We naively expected to work on them the whole shift. Then, like a stab of pain from a broken tooth we spotted Mr. Champagne again.

He was in his familiar, complete leather suit with "Champagne" emblazoned across his back. He was driving northbound down the middle of the road at a high rate of speed towards Fort McKay. Initially, we believed he had spotted our marked police car. His speed suggested he wanted to avoid another ticket. Since he was still driving, and it was Sunday afternoon, we knew he couldn't have insured the bike on the weekend back then.

A pursuit ensued. It took approximately four miles before we found ourselves alongside him. Gus rolled down his window and motioned at him to stop. After I engaged our emergency equipment, he looked over at us. The siren and lights only served to spur him on to a speed of about sixty miles per hour on the dirt highway. He seemed determined to get away. After about another kilometre he seemed to realize we weren't going to give up.

In the interest of safety, we only kept up the chase as no one else was on the highway travelling in either direction. The pursuit continued. The road on that stretch became very rough with many deep ruts. Mr. Champagne had taken action by moving over into the right-side ditch, as it was much smoother. He increased his speed. I maintained our parallel pursuit hoping he would gradually come to his senses.

Suddenly, Gus yelled, "Drive up beside him! I'll stop him!" I didn't quite know what he planned to do, but I trusted his judgement. I slowly moved my car to the right, closer to the motorcycle. I was driving half on the roadway and half in the smooth ditch about two feet from Champagne. I momentarily looked down at my speedometer and noticed Champagne had slowed to about forty-five miles an hour.

Without warning, the instant I looked over at the motorcycle again, Gus opened his door and slammed it directly into the side of Champagne's bike. I jammed on the brakes upon hearing the sudden crash. We skidded some distance along the ditch. I purposely turned my wheels so it would bring my car back on the highway again. Simultaneously, I watched the tumbling debris of Mr. Champagne who seemed to be enveloped within a cloud of dust, rocks, and small pieces of his flying motorcycle. I gritted my teeth as my car came to a sliding stop.

I turned around as quickly as possible and returned to the crash site. I looked at Gus; he was pale as a ghost.

I blurted out, "Why the hell did you do that?" He opened his mouth in response, but nothing came out. We exited the car and ran towards the rider who was lying on his side in the ditch. Before we got to him, he bounced to his feet in a fighting stance. His bike was lying in pieces, but Mr. Champagne had survived the crash unscathed. Our focus immediately moved from his possible injury to a possible confrontation. Influenced by the surprise of the accident and the effects of adrenalin, I yelled at him.

"Why didn't you stop? You now face a Fail to Stop for a Peace Officer charge!"

At that he took a swing at Gus. The whole thing seemed like a movie where the bad guy didn't want to be taken alive. The fight went on. Both of us jumped in to subdue him so we could affect an arrest. All three of us found ourselves on the ground. I was busy attempting to prevent him from punching by holding his arms and legs. Gus held him in a choke-hold with one arm while trying to remove his helmet with the other.

Suddenly, we heard a voice from above.

"Can you boys use any help down there?"

The fighting action stopped immediately. We all looked up at the same time. To our surprise, our local judge was standing on the side of the road above us. He was holding his cane in his left hand for support. Both Gus and I were astounded. There we were out in the middle of muskeg country and "at the end of the road" as Champagne would say.

Thoughts went through my head.

What were the odds that our judge would be way out here? He had just witnessed our takedown method. It was a situation that I had yet to deal with. In addition, he had just offered to help us—a man who needed a cane to walk!

Gus and I simultaneously yelled, "No Sir! Thanks anyway!"

We listened as he calmly replied, "OK, then I'll be on my way."

We all watched in silence as he disappeared away from the edge of the fairly deep ditch. Mr. Champagne had stopped fighting Gus and pulled his helmet off. When the judge was out of sight, Champagne spoke first. He was a bit dazed from the crash but more so by the sight of an elderly man with a cane stopping to help the police.

"Who was that?"

Like two singing choirboys we gave him the definitive answer.

"He's the judge who's going to hear your case tomorrow!"

The trouble was over just as abruptly as it began. Mr. Champagne was arrested and placed into the rear of our car. His motorcycle was impounded along with the scattering of detached parts. Gus and I returned to the office to process the charges against Mr. Champagne.

The next morning, he was brought before the same judge. When asked his plea, Mr. Champagne surprised us by pleading guilty to all charges. He was released on foot after receiving a $1,000 fine in total. That included charges for no insurance, failure to stop for a peace officer, and assaulting a peace officer.

When Gus and I walked out of the court, I said, "Gus, we got to talk about this door-opening thing!"

CHAPTER 42

Hidden Factors

I STARTED ANOTHER HIGHWAY PATROL shift with thoughts that the day would be like any other. For the last several days, it had been a cavalcade of routine speeders with the odd liquor ticket thrown in for good measure. It was also another grand sunny morning. I felt I had everything to live for and nothing really to gripe about. It was getting close to the noon hour. I was neither bored nor tired. I was wide-awake with the feeing I was ready for anything.

It was shortly after 11:35 a.m. when I spotted a lone female driving in a red convertible with its top down. I received three definite speed-readings on my moving mode radar set indicating that she was twenty kilometres per hour over the limit. I took up the pursuit immediately. Within a couple of kilometres south of Fort McMurray, I successfully stopped the vehicle.

The female driver was not alone. She had a medium-sized German shepherd in the back seat of the Chrysler Sebring. Upon opening my car door, the shepherd jumped towards me, positioning himself by placing his front paws on the rear trunk area of her car. It stood with its lower half on the back seat seemingly ready to attack. It had begun to bark and growl incessantly, threatening to spring from the car at any moment. Before approaching the rear of her car, I called out to the woman to hold on to her dog. She looked back at me without uttering a response. I began to close the gap between the car and myself. I repeated the message. Her casual response was, "My dog won't hurt you!"

When I got approximately two feet from the left rear side of her car, she repeated it again, "My dog won't hurt you!"

The dog seemed even more agitated when she spoke. I knew my concern was valid. My instincts were correct. It jumped and lunged at me. I stepped back several steps as quickly as possible to avoid a bite. Try as it may, the dog couldn't quite get its hind legs out of the back seat so it couldn't quite reach me. I stood approximately three feet away from the driver's side door. The dog continuously bounced from the trunk to the left rear side of the woman's car in its quest to attack.

Its growling and barking became even more vicious. It had been so aggressive in those few seconds I watched it leave scratch marks in the paint on her left rear door and on the rear trunk lid of her car. It persisted in trying to get at me. I couldn't realistically reach for the woman's particulars without getting bitten. I repeatedly asked the woman to hold onto her dog.

There was no way I was going to allow the dog to bite me. Especially, if it was just to prove a point that Mounties were brave and somehow stupid. I knew I had no choice but to deal with the matter.

I had to be polite, yet as firm as possible. I didn't want the event to escalate into something much worse. After all I had been bitten by a dog before. I remembered the bite through the hand as I was dragged from my car back in Vermilion by another ill-tempered German shepherd. We all know how that ended.

I maintained my stance, still determined to get through to the woman. I repeated an expanded version of the message once more. "Please, hold on to your dog! If it bites me, I may have to shoot it! Hold onto your dog! Please!"

After several yelled repetitions of the message, it finally got through. I must have sounded angry because her sudden reaction was abrupt. The gravity of the situation became crystal clear. She grabbed her dog's collar and pulled it into the front seat. She repeated angrily, "My dog won't hurt you! My dog won't hurt you!"

I thought telling her the truth was the proper thing to do. It wasn't my intention to scare her, just force her to secure her dog.

She remained angry with me the whole time it took the incident to be over. I really never did understand why she was so angry. I distinctly remembered thinking, "How can she be angry? I should be the one that is angry! She is creating this potentially dangerous situation!"

I felt she should have subdued the aggressiveness of her pet long before I had even approached her car.

Shortly after the dog was placed under control, I went into the polite business mode, as everyone deserves. That goes for everyone, regardless of whether or not they're angry with me. I had always used the same method for all ticket transactions so I would be consistent for court purposes.

My politeness didn't seem to affect the dog's behaviour at all. It barked continuously throughout the transaction. Even though its master held it tightly to her side it lunged towards me at every opportunity.

I remembered noting how strange it all seemed. The woman hung onto the dog as if she was trying to save its life, and the dog acted like it was trying to save her life. Both acting in good faith, I suppose.

At the time, all I really knew was I needed to enforce the traffic violation. With a look of disgust, she reluctantly produced her documents after I explained the reason for the police stop. She had no questions, nor did she give any replies.

I returned to my car to write the ticket. I kept looking up several times half expecting the dog to be climbing my door. The incessant barking was loud and annoying. Even so, each time I looked up I couldn't help but notice her demeanor. She just sat staring straight ahead, stone faced holding onto her barking dog. At that time, I lacked the intuitiveness and experience to recognize the possible causes for the symptoms she was openly exhibiting.

I returned to her car within a few short minutes. The dog was still barking and pulling viciously in an attempt to be released from his master. There was no doubt it wanted a piece of me.

I explained the ticket to her politely. I saw no facial reaction from her as I passed her the ticket. I returned to my car looking back periodically to ensure she hadn't purposely sent her dog after me.

Minutes later, after travelling several kilometres down Highway #63, I still wondered why she acted so strange.

I couldn't justify it so I finally told myself I wasn't out there to psycho-analyze every person I stopped.

With that settled, I moved on to the next clients. I had worked through the lunch period and into the early afternoon. Overall, it had been a good day.

I had just sat down to tally up my tickets and overall contacts when the operations N.C.O. asked me to attend his office. I immediately replied, "Is there anything wrong?"

He responded, "A woman came in earlier with a complaint about you. She said that you had threatened to kill her dog. I guess that you stopped her a short time after she received the bad news from her doctor. She was advised that she had cancer. So, Tim, come into my office and tell me what happened?"

I followed him to his office. I proceeded to repeat the complete incident. I reassured the operations NCO I had no idea she had just left her doctor's office. She hadn't given any hint that she had a serious, devastating disease like cancer. I told him my one strange observation was that she seemed a bit dazed. Not the drunk kind of dazed but the look of someone wanting to be anywhere else other than where she was at the moment. I had thought it was how she handled getting a ticket.

I suddenly heard my own words. I probably should have queried her on what was wrong. After all she hadn't exactly acted like the other violators I had dealt with on that day. He accepted my explanation but went on to explain that the complaint would have to be investigated thoroughly by our people in Edmonton, as per the policy.

I fully understood the woman's response during the stop. I even understood her protective pet's reaction. The dog must have felt all her pain and fear too but didn't know where it was coming from. It was only acting to protect her from the unknown fear she must have projected. I felt sadness for the lady.

On the other side of the coin, I hadn't done anything wrong either. I can only admit to you I was not impressed with the staff sergeant's response. With all his experience he should have put two and two together and got four. He knew me. He also knew how I treated violators. It was no secret I strived to be fair and compassionate when the circumstances dictated that course of action. I was angry at two things. Both angry at myself and at the staff sergeant.

I was angry at myself for not recognizing her zoned out state and for not querying her on her situation. I was angry at the staff sergeant for letting a simple misunderstanding create a complaint that would go on my record. The staff sergeant should have had the experience to understand why she was making the complaint.

Even with my limited service in the Force it was very plain to me as a human once I heard her devastating news. At the time, I believed my N.C.O. should have and could have taken a moment or two to determine why she was really angry. Was it my demeanour or was it the recent news she was terminally ill with cancer? I suddenly realized our recent traffic encounter served only to heighten her fears.

Hearing my threats to remove her dog from life was the last straw. Her dog was her only support for what she feared would be inevitable. It would be the needed companion she would count on during her illness.

Information gained after the investigation was complete revealed she was single with no husband or children. She had no support system. She must have felt so alone and betrayed by life.

She was told she had terminal cancer approximately a short ten minutes before being stopped by me. Nothing could be done. She knew she was going to die of cancer. If I shot her dog, she knew she would die alone. For her it was the last straw.

It was understandable why she thought my actions were inappropriate. Nevertheless, I was acting appropriately while carrying out my duty during a lawful vehicle stop. Just the threat while completely alone, and after having to face the terrible news all alone, it explained why she felt my threatening her dog's life was inappropriate. As for why she was angry at getting a ticket, I thought that after giving my explanation, he would see I was innocent of any wrongdoing, then quash the complaint. Unfortunately, some of my misunderstanding was due to my lack of knowledge of the ever-changing Force policies. Working in Fort McMurray didn't afford much time for casual reading of the Administration Manual.

My lack of knowledge aside, it really hadn't stopped me from feeling guilty for not recognizing her predicament. I had always been proud of myself for trying to treat everyone with respect and with fairness.

Before I was to leave highway duties in Fort McMurray, I would come to realize receiving complaints from violators was nothing more than a normal part of the process. Complaints were a given on traffic duties. After all, I was stopping regular people for committing what some regarded as very minor offences. Some believed that the federal police force of Canada shouldn't have been enforcing traffic laws. Nevertheless, we were mandated to do so in Alberta.

But at that moment, I felt differently. I knew that I acted appropriately, so I was dismayed at the action that had to be taken. *Why wouldn't the Staff Sergeant take my side and quash the complaint? Was it the fact that the lady had cancer?*

I hadn't known then, but during that specific time period the Force's policy regarding complaints against members had changed. The new policy effectively took away the ability of the local NCOs to investigate or conclude complaints.

The only way I saw I could have avoided the complaint was to have either taken a bite from her dog or queried her on what was wrong after threatening her dog. Either way it seemed like a no-win situation. Was it even my place to ask her personal questions dealing with medical problems?

I wrestled with those questions and many more that night. Finally, I came to the only logical conclusion: I had acted in the appropriate manner considering the chain of events that evolved. In saying that, deep down I knew my action had made matters worse from the standpoint of a potentially dying woman. How cruel she must have thought I was for issuing her that ticket.

I was able to convince myself that I was still comfortable with the enforcement side of police work. I knew I had to go on realizing occasional misunderstandings would occur between violators and members.

Finally, after over-thinking the incident, I had mentally accepted the inevitability of the process that had to be followed. There was nothing more I could have done as actions had been decided long before I had returned to the office on that date.

It had given me a wake-up call though. I began to take the time to read the "green sheets" and the Administration Manual so I would never be blindsided by changing Force policy again. Far too many of us had just gone out and worked, shunning the administration side of the Force.

Until then, I had felt that it was a sergeant or corporal's job. I had enjoyed the work as a regular constable so much that I neglected to be too concerned about how complaints were handled. That simple incident made me painfully aware that it was incumbent upon me to be familiar with all procedures.

The first week after the complaint was difficult for me, but with week after week of steady work, the complaint faded to a distant memory. Until one day, I was talking to one of our administrative stenographers. She had gotten to know me fairly well. I had concluded a large number of self-generated files by then. She had been tasked with reading the members' concluded files to ensure the quality of investigations was kept at a high standard. I must have done something right, as she was always friendly to me.

After a short duration of pleasant small talk, she asked me, "Have you seen the results of that complaint against you about the woman and the dog?"

I knew right away what she meant, and I responded, "No! No one has told me a thing about the final results of the investigation"

"They should have. It was returned to us at least two months ago. Your corporal should have told you the outcome."

I watched as she opened the file. "Yes, here are the results." She handed me a piece of paper from the file.

It was a letter that had been sent to the complainant from the commanding officer of "K" Division. To paraphrase, it basically stated that after a thorough investigation was conducted, it had been determined that Constable Mitchell acted appropriately when considering all the circumstances involving your dog not being properly tethered within the confines of your vehicle.

I was relieved and a bit upset at the same time. It was just a little thing, but that was the first time that I had realized the system sometimes failed.

Why hadn't I been notified two months ago?" I kept thinking, *I had only been notified by luck! By chance! And by happening to know someone connected to that knowledge!*

I thanked her and asked for a photocopy of the letter for my records. She graciously complied.

That complaint had been only my second one since I had joined the Force. My first complaint had been previously related to you in "The Pickup Line" story. But the dog complaint had clearly stayed with me all these years.

I have had many more complaints during the course of my career. None had affected me as much as that particular one. My previous attitude of complete trust in the system to do the right thing changed to a more realistic, guarded view.

I started to take a keen interest in the administration side of the Force. From that time onward, I remained vigilant to learn and understand Force policies. It would be that informed use of administrative knowledge that would protect me like armour whenever I was wrongly accused. Whether it be accusations made by angry complainants hoping to escape the results of a ticket or a charge, or even a complaint from another peace officer.

CHAPTER 43

Heading South!

THE SUMMER OF 1980 HAD come. Four busy years had elapsed. In retrospect now, it seemed to be over in the blink of an eye. My exposure to the numerous and varied types of investigations had produced professional and personal challenges that I couldn't have experienced in a more southerly, quieter detachment. I had often said to others later that my exciting years at Fort McMurray had most likely afforded the same experience I might have gotten working ten years in a small-town detachment down south.

It was an experience that came with deep personal rewards. I had survived the plane trips to Edmonton escorting prisoners, the jet boat rides up and down the Athabasca River, the many fights, and the verbal confrontations from bar brawls and arrests. I somehow survived the many potentially dangerous family disputes and the countless hours of working alone against the odds. A fact we shouldn't even mention. The time spent in Fort McMurray also gave me a greater understanding of the brotherhood of the Force.

It instilled a real sense of camaraderie for me. The very kind that develops between individuals who are forced to work long hours together on dangerous projects that require teamwork by virtue of their chosen career. The magic of permanent bonds between individuals becomes the final result. It was a result that can only be produced when men and women engage in providing protection for each other in desperate situations. I left there an individual proud of being a member of the Force.

I was blessed with the luck and the common sense to have been able to bring most incidents to a successful outcome. Of course, on rare occasions, I experienced failure. I could do nothing but deal with those specific times in my own way. Those seemed to have been the times when it didn't matter whether I used all my strength and investigative powers, the outcome appeared to be pre-ordained.

The day came when the officer-in-charge of Fort McMurray recommended I be transferred to a more southerly posting. He had set the wheels in motion for a transfer to a completely new duty with Airdrie Freeway patrol.

During my time at the Fort, I had also gotten married to a girl I met in Fort McMurray who was originally from Summerland in British Columbia. We had one son who was born there. All my previous transfers had been straightforward because I had been single. All I had to do was pick-up a non-accountable payment cheque to cover a few meals and gas, load my personal vehicle, then drive to my next post.

Having a family with two dependants complicated the transfer process to Airdrie. I was suddenly inundated with reading material that was unfamiliar to me. I was introduced to the Force's complex transfer and allowance policies. They dealt with everything from benefits for each dependant, buying my first home, and dealing with the moving company to obtaining my first mortgage and lawyer's fees.

Initially it was an overwhelming experience. If I had understood the process correctly, a member was expected to sell, move, and then take possession of a new home within specific time constraints. The transfer with a family was a finely choreographed spectacle of time and space full of stress and luck! Absolutely everything had to mesh to become a success. The timing was crucial.

As much as it was serious to me back then, I realized several moves later that no matter what difficulties came up during the transfer process, things always worked out. The biggest obstacle I had to get my head around was the timeframe imposed by the Force to complete their agenda—when to buy, when to sell, and when to take possession at the new post. It initially seemed overwhelmingly stressful and very complicated. Gradually the sense of stress would subside when I learned the specific job requirement, became familiar with the local area, and made new friends. Of course, other factors, like my wife finding a job and the children making new friends and settling into a new school environment, were other concerns. With every move the stress would become less and less until it became normal and exciting to move to a new posting.

Because the RCMP detachments across Canada were consistently understaffed, it was incumbent upon the transferee to immediately share in the caseload with an expectation to become an integral part of the team as soon as possible. In order to accomplish that, the member would be expected to learn the area and its people as quickly as possible.

Every place had its own way of doing things, so the new man was expected to ask when something seemed vague or wasn't understood. At some detachments, it was assumed that you should already know what to do in any circumstance. It sounds harsh but "trial by fire" created a quick learning process.

It all sounds barbaric, but there were many people in the detachment that provided solid, friendly advice even when you hadn't asked for it. With each detachment move the adaption process became easier and easier because of the continued experience one gained by working as a peace officer.

Airdrie, a bedroom community of approximately ten thousand residents was located about ten miles north of Calgary, Alberta, Highway #2. Airdrie Freeway patrol, as the name indicates, performed a great deal of self-generated enforcement-type investigations. When not checking drivers and vehicles for criminal code offences and provincial traffic offences, we investigated the many accidents that occurred along the forty miles of highway in our zone. I soon found that the duty was right up my alley.

During my previous stint with Fort McMurray Highway patrol, I realized I loved traffic duty. It was like I was meant for it. I had two things in my favour at my new post. Firstly, I had already learned the Alberta traffic laws inside and out. I was at a point where I could almost quote each section verbatim. Secondly, I had always enjoyed high-risk stops. The danger factor of not knowing the outcome of events with each vehicle-stop was exciting to me. It kept me on the cutting edge of interacting with the many individuals encountered each shift.

Don't misunderstand that admission on my part; I had never had a death wish. I had always employed all of the safety procedures that the Force had taught me. I just really enjoyed interacting with the unknown. I found I had always been able to work around problems, confrontations, and the sometimes-unbelievable personalities that travelled our roadways. It definitely was the unknown factor that made it for me. During my time with Freeway Patrol, I had always remained within the groupings of the top three enforcers of that unit. In those days, the number of contacts (violation tickets and written warnings) a traffic member would make each month was very important to the traffic supervisor. Once a year, we were assessed on the performance of our duties. The assessment was important as it helped determine who received a promotion, thus greater pay.

While on Airdrie Freeway patrol, I prided myself on getting an array of charges. I had always been one who gets bored very easily. I continuously sought out alternative charges as opposed to the standard speeding ticket. I found that the variety of criminal and provincial charges was endless when I just looked for them. To be more explicit, charges ranged from all types of criminal charges, drug charges, liquor charges, and wildlife charges, along with the usual traffic tickets and equipment violations. I picked up persons of every sex, colour, and nationality on warrants of all kinds. I thoroughly enjoyed the intermittent breaks from the mundane speeding violations. As strange as it seems, I really enjoyed it when a violator with a warrant developed. I liked the whole process of the arrest, the transport, and the booking of the culprit(s) into cells. In essence, it always gave me a chance to interact with that specific individual over a longer period of time. I had always been interested in humans.

I've always been amazed at what made them tick and what effects their cultures had on them, especially their behaviour towards our society and the police.

I was keenly aware that on most occasions it had taken very few people skills to communicate with a violator, especially when delivering some minor traffic offence on the road. Delivering and explaining a traffic ticket had routinely taken me from thirty-five seconds to five minutes at its longest. In that duration of time, I was consistently able to run the violator's particulars through the police computer, write the ticket, and explain it to the individual.

There were always exceptions to that routine. Those occasions would occur when an individual threatened, argued, or reacted in some violent way towards me. It included incidents where other evidence of criminal offences was being, or had been, committed by the driver or any of the vehicle's passengers during the vehicle stop. These greater investigations included offences like theft of motor vehicle, impaired driving, possession of narcotic or other contraband, and possession of stolen property, to name a few.

To investigate any incident to a successful outcome took time and the skillful use of a number of facets of police training in human nature. The understanding of social and ethnic customs; the knowledge and practice of proper interview techniques; an ability to read body language; and a degree of verbal expertise were all crucial aspects considered in the daily life of a Mountie on the road.

I settled into Airdrie Freeway patrol rather quickly. The guys and gals seemed great, and the work was exciting.

About the Author

Timothy Ian Mitchell

TIM WAS BORN IN MONCTON, New Brunswick. During his teens, he joined Air Cadets and by the time he was seventeen he had his pilot's licence. He had learned to fly gliders as well as fixed-wing aircraft. Upon graduating from high school, he joined the Armed Forces through the Officer Cadet Training Program and reached the rank of 2nd Lieutenant. A couple of years into the program, he decided that he would return to school and be trained as a machinist. He gained employment with Canadian National Railway. In 1974 he decided to apply for the RCMP and on June second, 1975, he was in Depot and after six months of training, he was posted to Vermilion, Alberta.

After that, he was posted to Jasper, AB, for Red Serge Duty, then to Fort McMurray, AB, where he performed municipal detachment, rural detachment, and highway patrol duties. After approximately four years, he was transferred to Airdrie Freeway patrol where he spent approximately ten years, culminating in becoming a technical traffic analyst. It was at this posting that he met his wife, Ivy-Anne, who helped him raise his two little boys, who were four and five at the time, along with her two children, who were ten and twelve. In 1990 he was transferred to Burnaby, British Columbia, where he became a forensic identification specialist. This involved training in all aspects of crime detection, from the development of trace evidence, blood markings, hair and fibre, fingerprints, footwear impressions, etc., to creating plan drawings and both video and photo re-enactments of crime scenes. As an integral part of this duty, technical training as a forensic photographer was required. After spending nine years of intense day-to-day practice, employing the photographic techniques that had been taught to him, he honed his skills by experiencing virtually almost any given situation a photographer could imagine.

He had been tasked with photographing all types of evidence. From the minute, almost invisible pieces of evidence, to capturing varying degrees of victim(s) personal injuries, under all conditions from sub-zero to pouring, rain to studio conditions. Experience included planned and controlled environments, such as award presentation photographs and identification badge photographs. For the duration of his thirty-two-year career he remained in the forensic identification field in different capacities, from an investigator in charge of several forensic units, to finally, a mentoring and teaching role.

This final phase occurred after his Parkinson's diagnosis during his tenure as the sergeant in charge of the Regina Forensic Unit. Just after being diagnosed with Parkinson's, he voluntarily removed himself from the investigative side of his duties to alleviate any possibility of loss of evidence at any given crime scene. Because of the disease, he could no longer perform the physical aspects of the job, for example, climbing, crawling, and finding evidence in precarious locations. This was supported by the CO of the division where Tim took up a new role of mentoring the younger forensic members, and his duties included being the scenes of crime officer's coordinator for the Province of Saskatchewan. Within this role, he was additionally tasked with developing and delivering the course to a group of SOCO candidates. Because of this teaching role, he was further engaged by the Canadian Law Enforcement Training Branch to give several one-day lectures on forensic identification to candidates of outside agencies that dealt with the Force.

In 2007 Tim decided to retire from the Force because he could no longer function to his expected standard because of the disease.

Retirement brought Tim and Ivy-Anne to Calgary to be closer to their four children and four grandchildren. Due to his love of photography, which he developed over the years as a forensic specialist, Tim put his newfound freedom into digital photography and mixed media art. In addition, he has put some of his other skills to work by creating many toys for the grandchildren, from an outdoor playhouse to an indoor tree-house, castle, dollhouse, etc. Many wonderful hours were spent playing with the grandchildren.

Since August 2009, and coinciding with a required increase in the total cocktail of drugs Tim needed to function properly, he started using acrylics to paint. Without any formal training, he has created approximately ninety paintings to date, painting almost daily. This has become such a passion that hours seem to pass in the blink of an eye for him. He sometimes attributes this new-found ability to the Parkinson's drugs he takes, like Mirapex. Sometimes he awakes during early mornings and attends to painting images that he had just dreamed about. Not all his paintings were created in this way, but a significant number have been painted after such dreams. He regularly sold his paintings as he had his artworks and photographs on display and for sale at our daughter, Julie-Anne's, JACC Fine Art Gallery in Calgary up until 2013.

After retirement in 2007, Tim became an active member of the Calgary RCMP Veterans' Association and spent many years volunteering his time at Fort Calgary, being their Photographer at all the social events, taking over doing the Newsletter, and being in the Calgary Stampede Parade with ten to twelve other veterans atop the Brewster bus. He thoroughly enjoyed all these activities until 2019 when he was no longer able to do them.

Printed in the USA
CPSIA information can be obtained
at www.ICGtesting.com
JSHW021932171124
73568JS00001B/8